INDIA FANTASTIQUE

ABU JANI SANDEEP KHOSLA

India Fantastique
Fashion

Text by Gayatri Sinha
PHOTOGRAPHS BY RAM SHERGILL
with 402 illustrations, 300 in colour

Thames & Hudson

We are blessed to have parents who let us fly and live our dreams. Thank you Ruby, Asghar, Pimi and DP. Love you, Abu and Sandeep

COVER: FRONT *Gold jewelled dress, hand-embroidered with pieces of metal inspired by South Indian gold jewelry, 2011.*
BACK *Off-white chaddar in khadi, with all-over gota embroidery, 2008.*

PAGE 2 *Aubergine kaftan with silver-grey sequin embroidery, 2009.*

First published in the United Kingdom in 2012 by Thames & Hudson Ltd, 181A High Holborn, London WC1V 7QX

India Fantastique: Fashion copyright © 2012 Abu Jani Sandeep Khosla

Text by Gayatri Sinha copyright © 2012 Abu Jani Sandeep Khosla

'The Golden Thread' text by Lubna Khan copyright © 2012 Abu Jani Sandeep Khosla

Photographs by Ram Shergill copyright © 2012 Abu Jani Sandeep Khosla

Photographs p. 12 bottom courtesy T. T. Barodawalla family; p. 14 Ajay Nayar; p. 18 Jagdish Mali; p. 21 Jagdish Mali, Deepan, Atul Kasbekar and Suresh Natrajan; p. 24 Shantanu Sheorey; pp. 26, 29 top, 278 top, 350, 351 Suresh Cordo; p. 28 top Denzil Sequera; pp. 28 bottom, 30 top Ashok Salian; p. 29 bottom Gautam Rajadhakshya; p. 31 top and bottom Mike Blake, Reuters, Popperfoto; p. 32 bottom Avinash Gowariker; pp. 256, 257, 258 left top and bottom Deidi von Schaewen; p. 258 right Ravi Kapoor; p. 276 Deepan; p. 366 Andrew Hiles; p. 367 Saurabh Dua. Any other photographs not otherwise credited are in the authors' collection.

Designed by Graham Rounthwaite Studio

British Library Cataloguing-in-Publication Data
A catalogue record for this book is available from the British Library

ISBN 978-0-500-51638-6

This is one volume of the two-volume *India Fantastique*. The other volume is *Interiors*.

Printed and bound in China by C&C Offset Printing Co. Ltd.

To find out about all our publications, please visit **www.thamesandhudson.com**. There you can subscribe to our e-newsletter, browse or download our current catalogue, and buy any titles that are in print.

CONTENTS

preface

A creation of Abu Jani and Sandeep Khosla is more a work of art than clothing. For me, Abu and Sandeep are the epitome of Indian couture, perfecting the art of beautiful dressmaking and intricate designing. My family and I have been fortunate to have the honour to wear their designs and to share a close bond with the duo. I have experienced for myself for many years the brilliance of their workmanship and their penchant for trying new designs and new details as they weave their charm and passion through the clothes they create for any occasion. Through sheer talent, passion and genius, every work of theirs stands out. No wonder wearing an Abu Sandeep ensemble makes one feel different in one's own skin!

It is the art of captivatingly blending the traditional with the contemporary that Abu and Sandeep have perfected. What this fantastic designer duo have accomplished with their pioneering contribution to Indian haute couture in the last twenty-five years has awed and amazed lovers of clothes and fashion alike. Flawlessly exploring an eclectic range of Indian tastes and ethnic apparels, and effortlessly catering to Western sensibilities, they have always shown their talent. Through their incredible chikan work and zardozi they have especially enhanced the beauty of ancient Indian arts. And when we know that they didn't have the benefit of formal training in their beloved craft, the value of their work becomes much more praiseworthy.

Beyond the realm of fashion, too, Abu and Sandeep have never ceased to amaze me. It has been incredible to see how the duo have expanded their horizons and made a mark in interior design and rediscovered aesthetic beauty in Indian furniture. I also had the joy of being on the inaugural edition of their television show *The First Ladies*, and the experience was one filled with their delightful sense of humour and fun. They made for impeccable hosts, and their eye for detail ensured excellence.

It is a matter of delight that Abu and Sandeep have ventured to capture the essence of their work in a publication. My heartiest congratulations to them for bringing out *India Fantastique* to commemorate the silver jubilee of a fantastic partnership! This magnificent book is both a celebration of style and a camaraderie that anyone would covet. Let the reservoir of their inventive spirit, alluring craftsmanship and brilliance in design continue to flourish always, with their legion of admirers ever looking forward to their exquisite offerings. I wish this book and every endeavour of Abu and Sandeep all success.

Nita M. Ambani

NITA M. AMBANI

foreword

Treat a work of art like a prince: let it speak to you first.
Arthur Schopenhauer, German philosopher

They walked into my house one morning, a shy smile on their faces and a world of expectation in their eyes. Jaya introduced them to me as Abu Jani and Sandeep Khosla, young men stepping into the world of couture, in the city of opportunity, Mumbai. They were very talented, the wife had gushed, an opinion she often takes ample time over before passing. I recognized immediately that they were destined to be our favourites, and I was not wrong.

As the days and the years have passed, 'the Boys', as they were endearingly referred to, have astonished me with the sheer genius of their creative art, not just in the field of design in clothing but in various other related and non-related creative acts.

Design to Abu and Sandeep has had manifestations in varied forms – the furniture in the house, interiors, an event; indeed in almost every aspect of life where aesthetics are up for a challenge. There has been, and I say this with some authority, a marked upward gradation in every enterprise of theirs. They were different, yes, but within the range of the high standards they had set themselves up to achieve. What one observed in their couture, one would not miss in their other accoutrements. The dignity, finesse and quality in the clothing reflected equally in the manner of their interiors, or any other artistry with which they associated themselves.

But what has remained most attractive to me has been their signature proximity to tradition and the culture of our country, India. Their belief in the exotic and unique, unexplored, timeless artwork in their land of birth has been astonishing. Discovering and exploring the myriad range of fine workmanship, and then embellishing it with their own, has been akin to adding ornamentation to melody.

'Mankind must never be too distant from tradition,' my father, Dr Harivansh Rai Bachchan, the renowned and distinguished poet and *littérateur*, wrote. Abu and Sandeep have always adhered to such belief. Their masterpieces have all been traditionally Indian and have succumbed in the most poetic manner within their creative forms. In the cacophony of couture excesses, their brand stands alone and distinct: close to the heart and the land.

It is only justifiable, then, that their exquisite journey of twenty-five years be encapsulated in a book, which you hold now. Some of the most prominent names associated with art, design and publishing have come together to bring out this most special and prestigious collection, commemorating the duo's exceptional contributions. In a world where the significance of documentation has rapidly shifted from turning silk-edged pages to opening network windows, this treasure trove is a most welcome and valuable diversion.

Abu and Sandeep have, through the years, entrusted us as a family by being a part of it. We are fortunate that such genius resides close by and within us. But even if this relationship had not existed, they would have, through their distinguished artistry, been a part of it.

I am honoured to have been asked to be a part of this enlightening publication, and I wish 'the Boys' continued excellence and even greater success.

AMITABH BACHCHAN

introducing
abu jani

The brilliant profligacy of the brand Abu Jani Sandeep Khosla had little beginnings. In 1979,
from his large family home near Metro Cinema in South Mumbai, 19-year-old Abu Jani took the
train to Xerxes Bhathena's design studio at Pali Hill, Bandra, crossing the fetid hot tracks of the
Mumbai local railway. In a garage with four tailors, he would work in 12-hour shifts, designing
for Bollywood leading ladies, often to extreme deadlines. The work had the urgency and
unpredictability of Mumbai's nascent understanding of style in the 1980s. 'It was a time when the
film rode on the hero, and the heroine could often be called at a notice of 24 hours. We would
design, produce and accessorize under great pressure,' recalls Abu.

This humble start marked the imminent rise of one of India's leading fashion designers.
With it comes a narrative of struggle and aspiration. Abu was born in Mumbai in 1960, the
second of three children, to Ruby and Asgar Jani. As members of the Dawoodi Bohra community,
the family was familiar with a particular blend of conservatism and modernity. Asgar Jani had
trained as a pharmacist, but felt compelled to work in his father's hardware trade. In this gesture
Abu Jani sees the seeds of his father's slow and irreversible decline and financial distress.

Abu's childhood inclination to sketch and draw was fostered by dyslexia, a reading
disability that was not recognized at the time. His natural affinity was pictorial and aural, and
school became anathema. He doodled in his exercise books, was reprimanded and changed
schools frequently, moving between Christ Church, St Xavier's High School and the Sir JJ Fort
Boys and Girls High School. At the last school, the art teacher Mr Patel opened a window of
possibility by encouraging Abu to draw and by sharing his own work. Patel's drawings were of
Radha Krishna or Sohni Mahiwal, romantic throwbacks to the Bengal school of art and the heroic
narratives of early Indian modernist art. As subjects, such paintings tend to have flowing lines and
idealized landscapes. Abu Jani's love for surreal floral designs, detail and intricacy, and the use of
watercolours, dates back to this early fascination.

Within the family, however, there were other pressing compulsions, and there was little to
fall back on other than their sophisticated, if idiosyncratic, talents. Asgar Jani specialized in making
models from matchsticks — houses, airplanes and cars. Ruby had an interest in embroidery
and knitting, subscribing to *Woman's Home* and *Femina*, which carried embroidery and knitting
patterns. Even at school, Abu had shown entrepreneurial and design initiative. 'There was a Parsi
lady in the Fort area of Mumbai, who did embroidery. Her daughter was in school with me and
suggested I meet her mother, Benaifer Davierwala. And so I sold my first khaka to her. It was a
freelance job and I was in the 8th standard.'

Abu describes the cultural ethos of Mumbai in the 1960s and '70s. It is a boyhood
recollection of the dazzling entry of the city from art deco colonialism into an era of pop
effervescence. 'Very distinctly in the mid-'60s there was the culture of the gymkhanas. There were
Plymouths, Dodges, Cadillacs, with glamorous women dressed in chiffon saris and pearls going to
gymkhanas, clubs and the Taj Mahal Hotel… Today they say that Western culture is taking over
the Indian ethos and fashion, but in those days, too, women wore Western clothes. There was
Madame Pompadour at the Taj Mahal Hotel, and Hollywood Tailors in a building at Kala Ghoda,
and they stitched the most fabulous Western outfits. Much later I was to use Hollywood Tailors
when I designed period costumes for Alyque Padamsee's *Evita*.

'What Mumbai — and the beauty of Mumbai — was, was the culture of so many different
people: Anglo-Indians, Parsees, Khojas, Bohris, Muslims, Sindhis, Maharashtrians, Gujaratis, etc.,
who made the city what it was. Colaba was the hippest area. English music wafted out from
every home, and rock 'n' roll at the Radio Club. It was very, very progressive and cosmopolitan.
There were Chinese hairdressers everywhere, and my mother and aunts used to frequent

(Above) Abu's father's aunt, Tara Barodawalla.

(Opposite) Top row: Abu's mother's side of the family (the Lightwallas), his mother seated far right; his father's side of the family (the Janis), his father back row, second from left. Second row: Abu at 19; Abu as a child; his beloved grandmother; Abu doodling. Third row: Abu's father at centre on his graduation from St Xavier's College; Abu and Sandeep with their dear friend Lubna Khan; Abu's mother in the 1950s. Bottom row: Abu's cousin Insiya with her husband Brian; Abu's best friend Ismail; Abu; Abu and Sandeep with Abu's sister Sabrina.

them to get their hair permed with a stinky substance. Near Regal Cinema there used to be a restaurant called Allabeli, where my uncle and aunt, MD mamu and Fizah mami, took me, and I was bedazzled to see my first cabaret.

'Then came the '70s and the arrival of my teens. With it came my uncle, AD mamu, and his early 20s! We saw the twist and the mini-skirts, with bouffants and Anglo-Indian girls who could not speak Hindi. Towards the mid-'70s my uncle became a hippy … and then came his music and his 45 rpm records, just like a scene out of the film *Hare Rama Hare Krishna*. I saw the different progressions of the culture from the '60s to the '70s through the transition of my maternal family, which was a reflection of Mumbai. The big Cadillacs and Plymouths became props for Hindi films… On Mumbai roads, cars like Fiats, Beetles and Standard Heralds replaced them, and so was fashion replaced with bell bottoms, frayed jeans and loose short kurtis.'

The Jani home was not overtly Bohri in its everyday preoccupations, but it bore some of the marks of mid-twentieth-century Mumbai and its aspirations to cosmopolitanism. Within the home, the elements of creativity were individual and inventive. 'In my early teens, my sister Saby was like my muse. I would dress her up. I styled her once to wear tennis shorts and a small T-shirt with heels. The idea behind my styling was that I wanted her to look international! She was my model for experimenting and styling. My designing clothes started out with designing wardrobes for my sister. When she got engaged, I designed all her outfits, right up until her wedding and the trousseau.'

A figure of inspiration within the Bohri fold was Abu's father's aunt, Tara Barodawalla, who modified Bohri fashion to look elegant and individualistic: Abu saw her as the epitome of grace and beauty. Conditions in his own home had become strained. His first job at the age of seventeen was distributing anti-corrosion leaflets at a petrol pump. After successive unsuccessful attempts to enter the JJ School of Art, he enrolled to study history at Mumbai's prestigious Elphinstone College, but then dropped out due to the demands of his job at Xerxes's studio.

In the 1970s and '80s, costume design for Bollywood was still not organized as an art form. It came into prominence when Bhanu Athaiya was awarded an Oscar for Richard Attenborough's film, *Gandhi*. Xerxes was a hard taskmaster and his studio was Abu's school of learning. While there, Abu worked on costume designs for films including *Duniya*, *Namak Halal* and *Saagar*.

Leaving Xerxes, he then freelanced with Patanwala Exports, a design firm that exported embroidery. It was Abu's job to design the swatches and oversee their execution. Simultaneously he freelanced for the English theatre, a thriving activity in Mumbai in the 1980s. Alyque Padamsee, flamboyant advertising guru and theatre maven, had seen Abu's work as costume designer for a musical, *Greased Lightning*. He appointed Abu to design the clothes for *Evita*, his successful production that brought together the theatrical and musical talents of Sharon Prabhakar, Alisha Chinai and Dalip Tahil.

In the early 1980s, a legion of housewives with aspirations entered the domain of the 'boutique', with occasional and formal wear, wedding trousseaus and what was loosely known as 'ethnic wear'. But to sustain their aspirations, these new boutique owners needed a fleet of ghost designers. Abu ghost-designed for various women. The established mode of boutique lines and exhibitions was demanding but well paid: Abu earned between Rs. 100 and Rs. 400 per design. He would give each of his boutique aspirants four to five designs a day, and enjoyed his substantial earnings. His designs were unfortunately not documented and have not survived.

While Patanwala had designated Abu an embroidery expert, his next step of working for boutiques earned him the title of designer. It was at this stage, in the mid-1980s, as he juggled multiple assignments, that he met Sandeep Khosla.

introducing
sandeep khosla

(Top) Sandeep's parents, Pimi and Dharam Pal Khosla, at their wedding reception.

(Centre) Sandeep's aunt and uncle, Urmila and Jung Sondhi.

(Above) "My aunt, Surjit Jaiswal [seen with Margaret Thatcher], was my first exposure to contemporary Indian art. She herself was something of a work of art, appearing and posing alone in a room full of mirrors…"

Separated by distance and time, the narratives of Sandeep Khosla and Abu Jani bear an uncanny resemblance. Up until the time that Sandeep travelled to Mumbai and met Abu Jani in August 1986, everything in his life appeared to conspire to move towards an intersection of destinies.

Sandeep Khosla was born in 1963 in Kapurthala, a former Sikh princely state with a strong Francophone culture that traces its history back to the eleventh century. In this town, with a slow rhythm and minimal Punjabi enterprise, Sandeep's father, Dharam Pal Khosla, an England-qualified engineer, was among the few wealthy and modern industrialists. D. P. Khosla's factory, which had made sirens and water pumps during the Indo-Pak war, had also launched a range of domestic fans named Sonu, after the infant son Sandeep. The family invested conspicuously in items of luxury, not the least of which were their cars and a private box at Jagatjit, the only cinema hall in Kapurthala, where Sandeep and his sister Benu were taken to see films every Sunday.

The children's mother, Pimi, belonged to Kapurthala; her grandfather, Rai Bahadur Durga Dass Puri, had served as Home Minister to the Kapurthala rulers. In an unusual twist, Sandeep and Benu were to grow up with an alternative home and a second set of parents. Pimi's elder sister Urmila and her husband Jung Sondhi were a constant presence. Urmila was childless and Pimi compensated by sending her children to spend every alternate night at Urmila's farmhouse in nearby Fazalpur. In times of distress, this layered parenting of a second home and its sprawling rural ambience took some of the edge off the family's circumstances. The other vortex of support for Sandeep was his mother's positivity and the unflagging faith of his sister Benu, who has been a constant presence. There was also an extended circle of aunts, female relatives and friends, which constituted a kind of zenana of shared confidences, nurture and comfort, chatter and tea over canasta and cakes. This circle of easy intimacy prepared Sandeep for his enduring conversations and some of his deepest friendships with women, across generations.

Post-Independence elite Punjabi families had a shared subset of values: the evening club, elegant dressing and an uncritical belief in top-rank boarding schools. At the age of seven Sandeep was sent to Welham Boys, followed by Doon School. During the holidays his overwhelming memories are of his mother's sparkling home, chiffon saris with brocade borders, an abundant table and entertaining, and the confidences of many aunts, slipping in and out of ennui and petulant despair.

Doon School has traditionally employed art teachers from Santiniketan and Kolkata. After Sudhir Khastagir, Rathin Mitra successfully managed the art department. Sandeep, who trained under him, recalls his own enthusiastic response to batik, tie-and-dye and other craft-oriented exercises in the curriculum. Doon School inculcated in him the dignity of labour, even as he recognized himself as being different, as being guided by an overwhelming desire for brilliance and success. During the summer vacations, his training under Rathin Mitra was supplanted by Pimi's relentless schedule. Under a traditional chitrakaar, or artist, Sandeep was taught to paint faces of the gods, building up a panoply of mythological figures. His mother's social circuit also included the home of Surjit Jaiswal, wife of a leading Punjabi industrialist, and a major art collector. In her home for the first time he saw a large number of paintings by M. F. Husain, his first exposure in a lifelong fascination with contemporary Indian art. Surjit Jaiswal herself was something of a work of art, appearing and posing alone in a room full of mirrors in her capacious home. Mirrors as a leitmotif, breaking and enhancing reflective surfaces, continually recur in the clothes and designed interiors of Abu Sandeep.

Meanwhile, D. P. Khosla's enormously successful business enterprise, Sonu fans, started to slip into family disputes. The family's dominance began to shrink and their wealthy lifestyle had to adapt to a new reality. The grand social swirl of Kapurthala slowly ground to a halt.

(Below) Sandeep's first design foray, worn by good friend Vivaka Kumari.

(Opposite) Top row: Sandeep and sister Benu as children; Sandeep in a Doon School photograph, 1975, fifth from right in the second row back; Sandeep and his mother Pimi. Second row: Sandeep "pigging out"; Sandeep and Benu in school; Abu and Sandeep, "God's chosen few!"; Sandeep getting massaged by Kamlesh. Third row: nephew Surya; a thoughtful Sandeep; Sandeep with Surya and niece Saudamini; mother Pimi as a bride. Fourth row: sister Benu with children Saudamini and Surya; "Bollywood dreams"; "Limelight!" Bottom row: Sandeep with nephew Surya, father DP, sister Benu, aunt Urmila, mother Pimi, friend Lubna and niece Saudamini; Sandeep; Surya and Saudamini as children; Sandeep with friend Lubna.

Both Benu and Sandeep left their elite boarding institutions for local schools; in the absence of cars, Sandeep walked to college. He took the changes in his stride. Even in adverse circumstances, family morale was buttressed by what in retrospect appears to have been a perpetual, self-generating optimism.

The city of Jalandher, with its close ties to Kapurthala and Sandeep's extended family, now offered a tenuous career option. The wider family had an interest in leather goods and manufacturing, so Sandeep went to train at the Central Leather Research Institute at Chennai, where he specialized in several aspects of the leather business – dyeing, carving on leather, and styling bags and wallets. He returned to Jalandher to work at the sports goods manufacturer F. C. Sondhi & Co., famous for its equipment for India's most popular sport, cricket. Each day Sandeep travelled from Kapurthala to Jalandher by bus. From the small stipend that he earned at the factory he bought fabric. He asked his mother's permission to convert a room in her house into a temporary design workshop. Working with a local Jalandher tailor, he had his first successful fashion exhibition, making his creative trajectory now visible to friends and family. Within a year he had quit F. C. Sondhi & Co. and relocated to Delhi, a significant move because it allowed him to share digs with his sister Benu. In what became a pattern for the next few years, he shifted and moved on rapidly when things did not appear to rise to the level of expectation.

At that time – the early 1980s – Delhi as the locus of government was dominated by cottage industries and their dazzling display of handicrafts. Sandeep had visited the state emporia and cottage industries frequently on trips to Delhi with his family. It was in the cottage industries' kind of aesthetic of hand-spun fabrics, miniature painting and hand-tooled and inlaid furniture that the city's notion of 'good taste' was generated. For a few months Sandeep commuted every day to Chandni Chowk, Delhi's wholesale market in the heart of the walled city, in an attempt to establish a trade in leather. However, he soon abandoned the effort of selling bags and wallets, and obtained his first job, for a buying house creating Western high-street clothes. Here he worked with the proprietor, Anne Campbell, who in 1984 took him to London for the first time. He also created Indian clothes that were strong on mixes of fabrics and a vibrant palette.

It was at this time that his fascination with performance and the stage became manifest. He joined Barry John's Theatre Action Group, the premier repertory for English theatre in Delhi, where he performed in the comedy *See How They Run* and designed costumes for the Irving Berlin musical *Annie Get Your Gun*, directed by John. At this juncture, Benu's wedding led to a frenzy of design. On a tight budget, Sandeep sourced material from Delhi's Shankar Market and Nehru Place, did a play on colours and gota, and executed her entire trousseau with a master tailor in Jalandher.

Sandeep also took his first step as a professional designer when he secured a counter at Appearances, one of Delhi's first design stores. Appearances had marked a maturation of the garage boutique: space was shared among designers to push beyond the prevailing Punjabi taste for kalidar kurtas and Kanjeevaram silk saris. Delhi in the mid-1980s was deeply entrenched in a pastiche of ethnic wear – a broad taste patronized by middle-class women across metropolitan North India. Sandeep called his 100-square-foot space at Appearances 'Limelight', and that is where he did his designing and tailoring. Here he tried different lines, mixing satin and velvet, and creating oversize shirts for women. However, even the most elementary shifts in styling were resisted. Within a year Sandeep was tiring of Delhi's provincialism and decided to move to Mumbai.

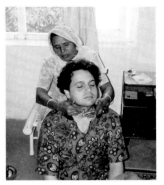

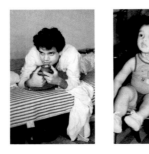

about the fashion

Mumbai in the 1980s was a city like no other. The explosion of new money coupled with massive industrial strikes had stretched and rent the existing fabric of the city. This once cosmopolitan centre of elegant clubs, poetry readings and a vibrant theatre and music culture was facing the prospect of a growing provincialism. In Bollywood, the mantle of the 'angry young man' had slipped from the shoulders of Amitabh Bachchan to a slew of middle-class metropolitan figures in the films of Govind Nihalani and Shyam Benegal's alternative cinema. Benegal's *Kalyug* (1981), a contemporary fictionalization of the *Mahabharata*, pitted two powerful business families against one another in a fratricidal war, enacted against the industrial backdrop of Mumbai. The new cinema under Benegal and Nihalini nudged out fantasy and wild make-believe and brought in the realism of the street. But art-house cinema had a niche audience. Amitabh Bachchan still ruled, as did Yash Chopra, Sanjay Dutt and Sunny Deol. Style was at a low ebb; the deglamorization of Bollywood was offset by social consciousness. The docks, porous with smuggled electronic goods, clothes, liquor and gold, became the field of D-Company; film producers paid protection money.

In the broad rubric of popular culture, the 1980s was a period of little confidence and less originality. Sandeep speaks of it as 'the worst period for Bollywood'; an era of synthetic materials and dubious Western designs on screen, and Hong Kong floral prints for women off screen. In the mid-'80s, an India without computers, colour television, IT hubs or malls, facing one of its worst ever financial crises as forex reserves plummeted, was forging a new template of urbanism. Mumbai, portrayed as vivid background in Salman Rushdie's *Satanic Verses*, was seen as a city of soaring wealth, deep sleaze and an uncertain future. The transformation of the essential character of the city during the '80s and '90s was witnessed by a host of other writers including Gregory David Roberts in *Shantaram*, Vikram Chandra in *Sacred Games* and Suketu Mehta in *Maximum City: Bombay Lost and Found.*

Abu Jani and Sandeep Khosla met on 15 August 1986. The meeting, perhaps predictably, took place at the studio of Xerxes Bhathena, which Sandeep had joined as a new boy (Abu was by now freelancing for many boutiques). On arrival in Mumbai in May, Sandeep had lived with a Doon School friend, Ajay Nayar, on Marine Drive and done the rounds by local train of the clothing stores. If Delhi was not willing to look beyond kalidar kurtas, Mumbai's preoccupations at this time were a kind of Indianized Westernwear in synthetic fabrics, the nadir of popular taste. 'Good taste', meanwhile, was dictated by a handful of powerful industrial families. A few stores in Delhi and Mumbai, such as Benares Silk House, Kala Niketan, Ravissant and Indian Textiles at the Taj Mumbai, had established themselves as the centres for quality Indian textiles and they put the product of the artisans within reach of wealthy buyers.

The nascent fashion industry of India, such as it was, evolved against the backdrop of the government of India's craft revival programme. In the larger context of nation, design as craft, as cottage industry and as aesthetic has had several resurgent avatars. Craft revival has moved in a steady arc from the avant-garde position of Kamaladevi Chattopadhyay (1903–1988) and her vigorous support for traditional artisans and the founding of a string of crafts museums (she spearheaded the major institutions of craft revival and distribution, such as the All India Handicrafts Board, the Central Cottage Industries and the Crafts Council of India, also guiding Weavers Centre, a highly significant initiative for artists, with alumni including K. G. Subramanyan, Arpita Singh, Manu Parekh and Jeram Patel).

Later the mantle of craft doyenne passed to Pupul Jayakar (1915–1997), who brought khadi into drawing rooms and persuaded women to exchange their chiffons for handloom. Jayakar had already sought to internationalize Indian handicraft. As head of the Handicrafts and Handlooms Export Corporation of India, she invited Pierre Cardin to India: he worked on a

new line with Indian textiles, pushing for the recognition of Indian handloom and introducing Anjali Mendes to Parisian fashion as India's first supermodel. Jayakar's efforts were a first step towards putting Indian designers on the radar of global design; they also carried the seeds of her gift to Indian design as the chairperson of the NIFT (National Institute of Fashion Technology) schools, creating an escalation in fashion consciousness. Jayakar's other great contribution was the Festivals of India. These events – a cultural arm for Indira Gandhi and Rajiv Gandhi – indulged in the kind of spectacularism that overturned the folk ethos of the Nehru–Indira Gandhi era and the blanched austerity and restraint of Gandhi's aesthetic values. The Festivals in Europe and America put design, folk art and craft, classical performance and contemporary art on the same platform of a contemporary context.

The Festivals of India template, and the integration of the arts and crafts, were to serve Abu and Sandeep well in their later massive design projects, as they excavated and then enhanced different artisanal forms. In the undocumented history of India's craft revival it is important to mark at what point government initiative slackens and individual genius and enterprise steps in. When Abu and Sandeep engaged with the crafts in a concerted way in the 1990s, it was against the already moribund edifice of institutional government structures and the complete lack of support of the individual designer. Their rise and impassioned craft revival was self-directed and entirely without government aid.

Abu and Sandeep's meeting at Mumbai took place against this backdrop of aesthetic aggrandisement. Their coming together of minds had a conclusive finality, centering on their hopes and desires. The meeting was decisive not least because it gave them a shared sense of purpose. Sandeep's parents had encouraged him to move on from Kapurthala with its now arcane feudal values; Abu was successfully freelancing but his ambitions were far from realized. After the first meeting at Xerxes, the pair met at Café Naaz at Hanging Gardens and walked until late at night, talking about their concerns around design, individuality and creativity, their goals and ambitions. Mumbai lay spread out before them, like a vast, darkened map with multiple illuminations.

As Abu says, 'Mumbai is a place of comfort. Mumbai as a city has given us freedom, a cosmopolitanism in our spaces. Mumbai has just let us be.' Within a month of their meeting, he and Sandeep had set up a partnership. In retrospect they believe that their own sense of urgent conviction and the volatile nature of the city tapped into one another. There was also a need to define, even through the smallest steps, their own goals. Abu's experience in selling a sketch a day and working at speed for films at Xerxes had led to a cycle of rapid designing and comfortable payment. For Alyque Padamsee's *Evita* he had produced sixty-five to seventy-five costumes, all within a minuscule budget. For the rest, he designed mainly for various boutiques across Mumbai. At this point a collaboration came about fortuitously. Gopi Mangnani offered to set up a boutique in Juhu, an offer that Abu shared with Sandeep. They agreed on a concept for the store. To this momentous venture they gave the name 'Mata Hari'.

The inspiration was an image of the dancer, courtesan and proclaimed spy from a set of Hollywood cards owned by Abu's father. Mata Hari, dressed in an East–West pastiche of an elaborate bejewelled bustier and exotic headgear, is the model for the cabaret star, the vamp, the 'wronged' woman. With her name, Abu and Sandeep announced their commitment to visual excess in every detail of their presentation, committed as they were to the understanding that 'there were no rules and no boundaries'. Sandeep adds, 'Money was changing hands. Whenever money changes hands, art flourishes. The new rich needed direction. We could lead.' The shop bags each bore a peacock feather; the trial room was circular to create the effect of changing under a spotlight; the walls were a shade of beige with a peach floor. Mata Hari marked the pair's

THE
Mata Hari
COLLECTION

A conspiracy of clothes
that flaunt the lyrical
sensuousness of the
legendary Siren Mata Hari.

Opening: Fri, 12th Dec, 1986
At 11 a.m.

3, MITHILA SHOPPING CENTRE,
J.V.P.D. SCHEME, JUHU,
BOMBAY 400 049, TELEPHONE: 573789

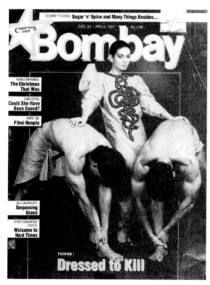

(Above) Cover of Bombay magazine,
featuring Mata Hari garments, 1987.

passion for 'pure' fabrics – chiffons, tulle, silks, organza – a commitment that they have adhered to throughout their careers. The clothes were India-inspired, but the cuts were Western, such as jackets with dhoti trousers and sari-inspired drapes with fitted jackets. For the first time, expensive weaves such as tanchoi and Jamevar were used. Surface embroidery and embellishment created the look and feel of refinement and luxury. The three-dimensional low-relief surfaces were in sharp contrast to the rough and flat embroidery available in the markets at that time.

Mata Hari opened with eighty garments, each of which was one of a kind. 'For the first time, the design element was introduced in a garment,' says Sandeep. At the time there was little or no fashion journalism, but Sandeep pushed for an interview with Mohini Bhullar, editor of *Bombay* magazine, in order to show her photographs of their work. Bhullar was impressed and granted them five pages and the cover before the opening of the store. Leading models Monica Dutta and Kitu Gidwani wore their clothes in the spread, shot by Namas Bhojwani in Roxy Cinema. Bhojwani's preference for monumental figures and dramatic frames against a chromatic background lent the photographs a keen visual edge. In this shoot we first see the partially nude, slick, copper-toned male figure and the regal, unattainable woman as a template that was to recur in the Abu Sandeep grand finale of the Delhi Couture Week in 2010.

Within days of the opening in 1986, the store window had caught the attention of a few of the leading lights of Mumbai. Dimple Kapadia, who had returned to cinema the previous year, was attracted by the store front and walked in. Jaya Bachchan and Parmeshwar Godrej also came, responded enthusiastically to the clothes and gradually became keen patrons and friends. Neerja Shah, head of Raymond's marketing division, invited them to create an entire line for the conglomerate, their first ever corporate commission. They were also approached to work on costumes for cinema actresses Rekha, Madhuri Dixit and Sonu Walia. 'To the shop came industrialists and film stars,' the pair remember. 'There was a whole turnaround of something new and a new concept in design.' Under the gaze of such attention, Abu and Sandeep created khakas in a spate, sometimes drawing and finishing two designs a day.

The Mata Hari experience seems to have created an image and an inspirational site that Abu and Sandeep returned to throughout the next twenty-five years. This was the figure of the courtesan-tragedienne, a figure rooted in climactic periods of history, evoking both desire and a lingering pathos. Nowadays, as masters of couture, of the grand gesture and visual spectacularism, Abu and Sandeep speak of their inspiration as coming from the historically constructed courtesans of Indian cinema: in Kamal Amrohi's film *Pakeezah* (1972) and K. Asif's *Mughal-e-Azam* (1960), and in the character of Chhoti Bahu, the neglected wife in *Sahib Bibi Aur Ghulam* (1962). However, the foundational template for the beautiful tragic figure lay in Mata Hari.

In *Pakeezah*, Meena Kumari as the beautiful tawaif, or courtesan, gained a tragic apotheosis in her own death, which occurred just few months after the release of the film. Kumari's personal tragedy melded with the Sahibjaan narrative and the film became a huge success. Its visual maximalism – deep reds, drapes and veils, chandeliers and rose petals – signalled the emotional excesses of the world of the Lucknow tawaif. These developed and played upon the luxury template laid out in *Mughal-e-Azam*, India's extravagant, popular, cinematic interpretation of love and intrigue in the Mughal court. *Mughal-e-Azam* spawned a mass cult of the historical as idealized romance. A new level of cinematic splendour was reached, with Madhubala as Anarkali, dancing in the Sheesh Mahal, or hall of mirrors. The biggest Indian box-office grosser until the advent of *Sholay* in 1975, the film tied beauty and tragedy together in a double bind. Taking a total of nine years to shoot, it saw the steady decline of Madhubala until her early death at the age of 36.

(Below) Meena Kumari as Chhoti Bahu in the 1962 production of Sahib Bibi Aur Ghulam, *directed by Abrar Alvi.*

(Centre) Meena Kumari as the courtesan Sahibjaan in Kamal Amrohi's Pakeezah, *released in 1972.*

(Above) Madhubala as Anarkali in the 1960 production of Mughal-e-Azam, *directed by K. Asif.*

Interestingly, the film drew a parallel with the kind of great pan-national craft tradition that both Kamaladevi and Pupul Jayakar espoused, and that later became evident in Abu and Sandeep's own design practice. On 5 August 2011, celebrating the film's fiftieth anniversary, the *Deccan Herald* proclaimed: 'The elaborate sets of Abkar's palace and choice of clothes of all characters were as authentic as possible… Tailors were especially hired from Delhi to stitch the costumes and specialists from Surat-Khambayat were employed for the embroidery, even as goldsmiths from Hyderabad designed the period jewellery. Kohlapuri craftsmen designed the crowns adorned by the actor, Rajasthani ironsmiths crafted the weapons and the elaborate footwear was ordered from Agra. A Lord Krishna idol in one scene was actually made out of real gold.' In a coincidence of aesthetic values, Abu and Sandeep have tended to draw upon strands of Indian craft style and unselfconsciously use them together, in clothing as much as in interior design.

The influence of Indian cinema in the domains of the imagination was echoed by the changing reality on the ground. Mata Hari attracted Bollywood's attention: Abu and Sandeep were commissioned to design clothes for film actresses Amrita Singh and Madhuri Dixit, for Sonu Walia in *Khoon Bhari Maang* and for Rekha in *Kama Sutra*. At this point their practice rapidly outgrew Mata Hari. In 1987, Tarun Tahiliani had returned from America, where he had trained at the Wharton School of Business. Tahiliani came to Mata Hari and offered Abu and Sandeep a space to work in his new establishment, Ensemble, on Mumbai's Dockyard Road. Ensemble was to be the first multi-designer couture store with a cluster of talented participants: Asha Sarabhai, Rohit Khosla, Niel Bieff, Anita and Sunita Kapur under the label Amaaya, and Anu M.

Abu and Sandeep chose to market their garments under the brand name Jashan. The word, which was an amalgam of their names, meant exuberant celebration. Each of their families had with great difficulty raised Rs. 50,000 each, so the duo had to make a success of the enterprise. In the 10 × 10-foot space that Ensemble had provided, they pushed to refine their practice further. The principle of using only pure materials, in contrast to the prevailing taste for industrial, synthetic fabrics, was to become their intrinsic approach. From Ensemble, they made their first trip to Varanasi. The sheer dazzling wealth of weaves that are unfurled on the white cushioned seating on the ground, and the feminine and luxurious nature of the work, can come as an epiphany to anyone visiting the fabric market there. Back in Mumbai, in the work room, one of the tailors accidentally spilled liquid on a silk garment. Abu washed it himself and left it to dry overnight. The next day the crushed garment appeared to have acquired its own beauty and tensile form. Recognizing an opportunity, Abu Sandeep created an entire line around crushed silk in strong earth and metallic colours. For many years crushed silk garments in combination with zardozi and other embellishments have been their signature.

Ensemble opened in December 1987, marking a new peak in Abu Sandeep's creative endeavour. Their collection had several firsts: silk crush skirts with tiny ghungroos, or bells, at the hem, and large-sized chaddar bandhini dupattas along with crushed bandhini. The churidar dogri pyjamas worn by the women of Himachal Pradesh, and familiar to Sandeep from childhood holidays in Dalhousie, were now transformed into churi-sleeved jackets. Potli buttons, made from tiny bunches of cloth, were also used.

In this period of dearth – no fashion institutions, no fashion week or magazines, no fashion critics – the tenuous thread of creative reputation was maintained entirely through social channels. At this point Neerja Shah took Sandeep to Sunita Pitamber's Artistic Boutique, where Jaya Bachchan was having an exhibition of khadi saris with Devika Bhojwani. Jaya, who had already bought their clothes at Mata Hari, introduced them to Pitamber, who then came for their opening at Ensemble.

(Below) Back view of Abu's sister Sabrina, modelling a crushed bandhani skirt, one of Abu Jani Sandeep Khosla's first outfits.

Ensemble was a colossal success, not least because it brought in Sunita Pitamber, fashion maverick and Mumbai's reigning hostess. She came with her own entourage of the rich and famous, as well as with the immediate promise of patronage. It was a moment of mutual recognition. When she died in May 2005, leading editor-journalist Malavika Singh described her passing: 'They were all there — ferociously stylish grande dames, top-flight decorators, ace designers, swish industrialists, die-hard bon vivants, A-list film stars and celebrated restaurateurs, all of whose lives had in some measure large or small been touched by a short, stocky, energetic woman, who many say taught Mumbai society how to live…'

Pitamber's entry into the lives of Abu and Sandeep was like gold dust on a wave of spectacular energy. She combined an international perspective with a highly located sensibility. The daughter of the leading gynaecological surgeon Dr V. N. Shirodkar (in 1955 he invented cervical cerclage, or the Shirodkar stitch), she was married to an erstwhile Rana of Nepal and successful businessman. As a prominent hostess, Vassar-educated art gallery owner and fashionista, she combined a contemporary sensibility with a keen sense of old cultural values. Always quick to recognize talent, she invited Abu and Sandeep to her home, where they met her entourage of Shakira Caine, Princess Ezra Jah of Hyderabad, Ira von Fürstenberg, Bianca Jagger, Princess Luciana Pignatelli and other social celebrities. 'The Boys', as they were dubbed, were meanwhile working at a manic rate.

'We were thrown into the stratosphere of the rich and the famous, catapulted into inventive channels of communication,' they recall. 'At the same time our principle was very simple. We would create only what we wanted to.' By now financial and creative differences had led them to leave Ensemble. Sunita Pitamber, in her role as catalyst, provided them the wherewithal to work. She offered her home in Juhu — called Sun-Pit — to double up as a workshop and she also marketed their clothing through Artistic, her boutique and art gallery. She poured her energy, networks and social heft into her projects — in this case 'the Boys', dressed in blue jeans and starched white shirts, their customary look for many years.

'She was a big influence,' says Abu. 'She took us on a whirlwind tour of style — antiques, textiles, jewelry, fine dining, arts and crafts, spectacular hospitality.' Shakira Caine, a close associate and friend of Pitamber, created the first opportunity for the pair to internationalize their designs. They travelled with Pitamber to London, where they were commissioned to design shawls for Harrods under the Shakira Caine brand. The shawls, which were made in naqqashi kania and saadi stitches, were a great success and marketed at Harrods and Harvey Nichols in London, and Bergdorf Goodman and Neiman Marcus in New York. Caine was inspired by an exhibition of Indian fashion at the Metropolitan Museum, not least because her great-grandparents were Indian. In collaboration with Pitamber, she created a collection of brocade jackets, belts and bags under her own label.

Expanding their presence in London, Abu and Sandeep began to retail at the store Joseph in 1989. In the same year they were invited by the organizers of a charity ball to raise funds for Save the Children, with a show at the National Trust property Osterley Park, which Princess Anne, a patron of the charity, attended. Back in Mumbai, Bina Kilachand of Areesa Gallery conceived of an art and fashion crossover, creating a show titled 'Art Wear'. The artists she invited to collaborate included Anjolie Ela Menon, Manjit Bawa and S. H. Raza. Abu decided to take transcontinental inspiration, creating flowing, heavily worked chaddars with figurative and geometric designs in black on white, inspired by the Maasai tribe of East Africa. His inspiration was a tribal neckpiece that Dimple Kapadia had just brought back from Africa. The heavily embroidered chaddar, much like a tapestry in itself, presented each model as a monumental,

(Below) Shakira Caine wearing a shawl and crushed jacket by Abu Jani Sandeep Khosla.

(Bottom) A model wearing one of Abu Jani Sandeep Khosla's shawls, sold at various luxury stores worldwide, under the Shakira Caine label.

timeless figure. The garments were worn over long flowing dresses, each using more than fifty metres of crêpe de chine, creating fifteen-metre flares. In later years Abu was to turn to the inspiration of the artist A. Ramachandran and create an entire series of objects, fabrics and designs around Ramachandran's leitmotif, the abundant lotus pond. The chaddar phase, however, was Abu Sandeep's first exploration of the area between art and fashion, in which the art gallerists Sunita Pitamber of Artistic and Bina Kilachand of Areesa brought their designs into the shared domain of the contemporary art world.

The difference between art and fashion is that, while art may celebrate doubt, fashion expresses confident certainty. Fashion, however, mirrors and draws on art. One of the foundational sources of Indian haute couture has been the legacy of Indian fabric that has come to attract documentation, archiving and the authority of museum collection since the mid-twentieth century. Thus Indian crafts are museumized, even as they are – in somewhat tepid or corrupted versions – sold in Indian bazaars. Museums such as the Sarabhai Foundation's Calico Museum, established in 1949, have had a profound effect on the curriculum of the National Institute of Design, Ahmedabad. The history of the Indian textile and its multitude of embellishments inspired Abu and Sandeep. 'Because we are untrained, nothing is impossible,' says Sandeep. 'We feel that the artisan is better than the design student. The movement away from the "pure" line can turn anywhere.'

The making of clothes, meanwhile, was also undergoing a quiet revolution. In small ways, the masculinist style of tailoring women's clothes was being replaced by references to history, to the smaller traditions of a regional palette and fabric. In 1989, for a show organized by Sunita Pitamber, Abu Sandeep created garments inspired by Indian miniature painting. For this they used semi-precious stones, glass and embroidered surfaces in the intricate and time-consuming marodi stitch. In another instance, in 1991, the skyline of Delhi, its ramparts, tombs and mosques, became a radical piece of design for what is described as their 'Architectural' line. As with Abu's other drawings, the architectural outline was evocative of medieval and Mughal India rather than any specific location. Just as the pair's interest in architecture was driven by an engagement with surface, so they actively pursued fabric and colour as fashion options. Along with cut and silhouette, it was also colour and fabric that were re-examined for an aesthetic context. One of these areas of unresolved usage was the colour white.

In India until the 1980s the 'single woman' was not the cognate term that it is today; rather it distinguished between the widow, the divorcee and the unmarried woman. Since antiquity, the colour of widowhood has been white, with its associations of grief and social ostracism. Bled of all tonality, it was associated with austerity. Mumbai cinema threw up rebels: Krishna Kapoor, the wife of Raj Kapoor, and his co-star Nargis wore white, attributed to Kapoor's love for the colour. Abu Sandeep, working with white on white for the Areesa Gallery 'Khadi' exhibition, gave the colour authority and plenitude. Later, inspired by the potential of white, and of white on white, they created an entire collection based on jamdani. A weave so ancient that it is mentioned in Kautilya's third-century text *Arthashartra*, jamdani is also referred to as an ancient export from India in the accounts of Arab and Chinese travellers. Woven in the Burdwan and North Bengal area, and traditionally used in saris, the material was adapted by Abu Sandeep for long kurtas with churidars, the natural elegance of the white fabric gaining a sensuous and generous dimension. Over time, in the range of whites, Abu Sandeep have used a clutch of weaves in Benaras, Dhakai and Kerala cotton and khadi.

By early 1993, Abu and Sandeep were on the cusp of one of the most significant changes of their creative partnership. They had decided to move out of Sun-Pit and Artistic boutique.

Shawl embroidered in jet sequins and bugle beads on coarse khadi fabric, made for the designers' 'Art Wear' collection.

Ink drawings by Abu of African-inspired women for the 'Art Wear' collection.

(Above) Amrita Singh, modelling an outfit from Abu Jani Sandeep Khosla's first jamdani collection in marodi cotton thread.

The label Jashan was replaced by Abu Jani Sandeep Khosla, and the pair moved into a two-room work and living space in the Shiv Shakti building in Juhu, from which they ran their workshop, their client relations, their lives. This studio-cum-living-space was to serve for several years as a roiling engine of creativity, and was a site of spectacular growth. The first public profiles of figures in Indian contemporary design were being drawn and Abu Sandeep were in the vanguard. In actual terms, Shiv Shakti was a protean space for living and working with a floating group of tailors, embroiderers and cutters. That 'India is so vast that it is a neverending source of inspiration' became a foundation for the pair's philosophy of value in design.

At Shiv Shakti, Abu and Sandeep were to evolve a rigorous and highly aestheticized approach to beauty and fashion. They structured a day-to-day approach to transforming their energy into work, to professionalizing their practice and to creating a working model of the freelance design entrepreneur where none had existed. 'Everyone we met was through our work,' notes Sandeep. 'Society accepts you if you are rich or famous or creative.' In their partnership, the intricate, highly detailed drawing was Abu's particular talent; Sandeep, who only sketches in broad strokes, believes he has the gift 'to magnify the dream, to take even a small element and create an entire collection around it'. By the close of the 1980s the Festivals of India were at the apex of articulating Indian design in the international space. For Abu and Sandeep, as distant but keen observers, there was the early realization that the festivals and the museumization of the crafts encouraged a belief in cultural obsolescence; that everything truly worthwhile belonged to the past. 'We were convinced that whatever had been done in the past could be done today,' says Sandeep.

In a charged and creatively explosive phase, living out of one room and working out of the other, they experimented with the concept of the sari, creating the double sari with two palloos, and the double dupatta. Whereas earlier they were committed to job work, now they entered the domain of retail. Today close to eight hundred employees work multiple shifts in the Abu Jani Sandeep Khosla factories, but it was at Shiv Shakti that their first experience of hiring hutment and kholi accommodation for their growing retinue of workers began. An enduring visual image of the Shiv Shakti days is of Sandeep driving around in his Maruti 800, gifted by his uncle Jung Sondhi, buying fabrics. 'Sandeep thinks faster than he can speak,' says Abu. 'Generosity and maximalism come from Sandeep. His vision is larger than life.' The pair did every aspect of the work together and the creative output from Shiv Shakti became multi-dimensional, spanning garments and encompassing the pair's first forays into furniture and interiors.

Abu describes the pair's early steps towards professionalism: 'We bought our first model form. In the absence of a formal education we experimented all the time. The inner strength that is manifest in fashion is different from art. We have to continually try a different signature.' While fashion retailing the world over has broadly depended on speedy and large-volume turnover, Abu Sandeep opted for slower rhythms and personalized clothing. Energy was invested in locating old masters of embroidery and learning from them. Abu's drawings on khakas drew inspiration from landscapes, kilims, Mughal architecture and floral designs. At Shiv Shakti the pair set up a factory-based practice, hiring their first galas, or industrial spaces, in Ghanshyam Industrial Estate in Andheri, its indifferent grey exterior in no way revealing the dreams being spun within. To any craft or embroidery connoisseur, the factory provided a mine of information on how traditional crafts are merged into contemporary couture. The factory also enabled Abu Sandeep's movement into the main lines of their practice: object and home design; a diffusion line for their stores; haute couture; and their vigorous entry into the luxury and clamour of the Great Indian Wedding.

(Below) A remnant of the massive fire that
destroyed Shiv Shakti in 1997.

(Above) Jaya Bachchan, wearing one of
Abu Jani Sandeep Khosla's earliest
chikan saris.

They created a landmark by designing a wedding reception outfit using gold Swarovski crystals to create a three-dimensional lotus pond. They also created a fashion show staged at Mumbai's Taj Hotel, presenting garments in silk and net with Swarovski crystals, and velvet with zardozi. Stitches, fabrics and embellishments, encompassing white khadi, the marodi stitch and the 'bandage' line, Balinese and flower power motifs on short kurtis, were created. The proceeds from this show were donated partly to the victims of the Latur earthquake, which had happened two days before the show, and partly to a children's home.

A massive fire in Shiv Shakti destroyed Abu Sandeep's clothes, research and drawings, compelling the closure of their living laboratory of ideas. The pair continued selling at Signature in Haus Khas, New Delhi, and they also started to edition their works into imaginative lines. That chikan travelled, lured and seduced with its beauty is witnessed by its international success. Through Sunita Pitamber, Abu and Sandeep met Eileen Coyne, an American jewelry designer, who in 1997 opened a shop called ALSO in London. She invited Abu and Sandeep to exhibit their clothes exclusively there, alongside her jewelry. She wore their clothes and promoted the combination of her designer jewelry with the high-fashion chikan garments. Her shop was located in Beauchamp Place in Knightsbridge, and its neighbours included Bertie Golightly, Jasper Conran, with his fabled simplicity in design, and Bruce Oldfield, who designed haute couture wedding wear as well as the McDonalds's staff uniform. The clothes in the ALSO shop window brought in acting divas and Academy Award-winners Judi Dench and Maggie Smith, along with Darcey Bussell, principal ballerina with the Royal Ballet in London, and Princess Michael of Kent. The ladies in white, all transnational stars, multiplied.

Sandeep says, 'I believe in God, and I believe we are God's chosen few.' Perhaps his conviction springs from the creative facility and the seemingly unending chain of artisanal genius that haute couture involves. The Abu Jani Sandeep Khosla factories in Mumbai are a microcosm of different strands of Indian craft traditions that, in making haute couture garments, continually redefine the craft itself, enhancing and altering its contours. As claimants of a tradition that they have painstakingly revived, Abu and Sandeep have also diverted, deflected and designed taste. One area of continual revival, revisited by craft and cultural historians, designers and craft revivalists, is khadi, a material that carries the imprint of nationalism and Gandhian values. At the apex of their evolution with khadi is their association with Jaya Bachchan. When they first met Jaya in 1987, she was on a hiatus from filmmaking and had created an exhibition of khadi garments with Devika Bhojwani at the Taj Hotel in Mumbai. Jaya's promotion of khadi garments had the strong recall of an electioneering campaign with Amitabh Bachchan for the Allahabad seat in the mid-1980s. Amitabh Bachchan went on to win the Allahabad Lok Sabha seat, but Jaya retained the memory of poor women in the villages of Allahabad, who wished for charkha spinning wheels to create economic self-sufficiency.

In the 1980s Jaya was already 'Guddi' to the nation – idealized ingénue with a bubbling innocence, the highly talented and then repressed singer of *Abhimaan*, and a slew of other credible filmic characters. Winner of several Filmfare awards, she was in 1987 six years past her last film (*Silsila*) and on an indefinite sabbatical. As the epitome of simplicity and 'good values', her film persona had ruled the hearts of India's masses – idealized daughter and friend, who negotiated modernity within the framework of tradition in a pre-globalized India. She also brought an unconscious educated sincerity to the Hindi film actress, stereotypically polarized between the heroine and the vamp.

As early meetings cemented into longstanding friendship, Jaya became for many the public face of Abu Jani Sandeep Khosla. She had already bought a garment from Mata Hari

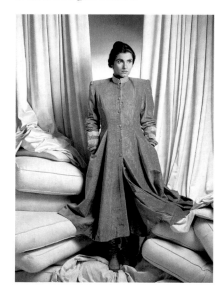

(Below) Dimple Kapadia, modelling the
first men's sherwani made for a woman,
in silver with gold borders.

(Above) Freida Pinto, wearing an Abu Jani
Sandeep Khosla outfit at the premiere of
the film Slumdog Millionaire in Leicester
Square, London, 2008.

but when the designers came to her exhibition she commissioned them to create clothes
for her, recognizing their talent as conspicuously different. 'She was ready to embrace a new
style of dressing,' they recall. It was for her that they made the first 48-panel kurta with three-
dimensional zardozi embroidery that dropped near ankle-length, dressing her in it for an
appearance at the Berlin Film Festival. A seeming contradiction for a short person, this kurta
became iconic and widely imitated. The perception around Jaya Bachchan gradually shifted
from her fictional persona in the films Guddi and Mili to her real-life persona as chair of the
Children's Film Society, jury member of the National Filmfare awards, and Member of Parliament.
For her role as chair of CFS, Abu Jani Sandeep Khosla did an entire line of khadi and zardozi
festival saris, which became her public trademark. They created saris with solid colours in khadi,
Bhagalpur silk with its rich metallic colours, khadi silk and twill, and woven saris with borders.
Jaya's enthusiastic support for their work – as much as for the charkha weavers of Allahabad
– was because she strongly opposed the government's official support for polyvastra, a blend
of khadi with polyester (in 2010, the cabinet in fact sanctioned a budget for the marketing of
polyvastra). In contrast, Abu Sandeep had designed the successful 'Joia Jalli' line of natural organic
wear, inspired by Jaya.

Jaya became their lady in white, commonly appearing in Abu Sandeep chikan or khadi
garments. By extension, the Bachchan family absorbed and reflected this style – part nationalist,
part haute couture. As their daughter Shweta grew from 'an awkward aspiring intellectual to
a fashion icon' they also created her clothes. Both Shweta and her brother Abhishek wore
white at their weddings, Shweta in chikan, Abhishek in white cotton, while the family wore
khadi. On occasion, Amitabh Bachchan has also worn their clothes on the ramp and specifically
commissioned their designs, as he did for the film Khuda Gawah. With Shweta's daughter Navya
Naveli, Abu Jani Sandeep Khosla now dress and style three generations of the Bachchan family.

If Jaya Bachchan, with her strongly individualistic personality, represented one kind
of iconic muse, the other was Dimple Kapadia. What khadi was to Jaya's intellectualism and
simplicity, zardozi was to Dimple's sensuous beauty. For many years Jaya wore the first of every
collection; now both Jaya and Dimple wore the clothes six to eight months before a collection
was released. When Abu first met Dimple, it was as an anonymous and unsung assistant to
Xerxes. He was the bearer of garments for her film Saagar (1985) and was struck by her beauty.
Dimple, meanwhile, was the phoenix rising, the tempestuous star of Bobby returning to cinema
after two children and a broken marriage, leaving Bollywood agog with speculation. Abu and
Sandeep, recognizing her independence, saw her personality as 'nomadic and unpredictable,
highly visible in her freedom'. Like Jaya, Dimple had patronized Abu Sandeep in Mata Hari
without knowing who they were; now she became central to their design fantasy.

Creating clothes for cinema stars within their roles, and for social wear, are two different
trajectories: the first involves cinematic character, the second individual personality and style.
With Dimple Kapadia, both of these categories merge, for she wears their clothes both on
screen and off. Abu Sandeep designed clothes for her film Pati Parmeshwar, and collaborated
with her sister Simple in creating her wardrobe. Numerous media shoots and magazine covers
were created around her, and Abu and Sandeep delighted in playing upon her beauty and her
individualism. 'I started wearing Abu Jani Sandeep Khosla around 1986,' says Dimple. 'The entire
styling and play of colours is what drew me. Their clothes can make even a regular woman look
special. These were the kind of clothes that I would like to wear. This is what I wanted to possess.'
Both Jaya and Dimple speak of the manner in which the clothes drape and cover the body; their
acutely feminine feel. 'There is a great sense of grandeur in their garments,' says Dimple. 'There is

also a lot of modesty.' Jaya, in turn, sees this as Abu and Sandeep's humanity and inherent respect for a person.

Within two decades of their practice, the Abu Jani Sandeep Khosla label had acquired a legion of admirers, including close friends like the actress Amrita Singh, with her highly individual sense of dress, as well as industrialists Lakshmi and Usha Mittal, and the Ambani family. As early as the Shiv Shakti days, Nita Ambani would visit the designers' space to source clothes. For Kokilaben Ambani's 75th birthday Abu and Sandeep arranged a private fashion show. They dress Mukesh and Nita Ambani's children, thus three generations of the Ambanis and also the Mittals.

Over the years, as their haute couture label has proliferated, Abu Jani Sandeep Khosla have greatly extended their sphere of influence. In 1998, they were invited to stage a fashion show over three floors of the National Gallery of Modern Art, Mumbai, to mark the end of 'The Enduring Image', a mammoth exhibition from the British Museum collection, presented by the British Council. In 2000, the conjunction between fashion and theatre was spectacularly conceived in a presentation in Mumbai's Famous Studios. Abu and Sandeep used the event to establish a fund for the NGO Ashray to support women and children affected by HIV/AIDS. The show was called 'Celebration of Style', and for the first time Bollywood actors Amitabh Bachchan, Abhishek Bachchan, Sonali Bendre, Raveena Tandon and Rahul Khanna walked the ramp in support. In 2005, the pair's architectural inspiration, directly manifest in their clothes, became the focus of the annual Jaipur Festival show, when the government of Rajasthan invited them to the Albert Hall Museum. They designed a 'Pink City' collection, in various hues of pink, and embroidered wall hangings detailing life and art traditions in the beautiful state of Rajasthan.

Central to the Abu Jani Sandeep Khosla brand of fashion is the city of Mumbai. As a muse and a massive cauldron of invention, the city continually revisits notions of time and space. Invoked in the creative imagination, fuelled by a million narratives, is this once great city, whose grandeur appears to be slipping away. 'At the heart it is Mumbai,' says Abu. 'Everything else is a window from the outside for me.' The manner in which the pair's lived experience filters into a design phenomenon is at the core of contemporary Abu Jani Sandeep Khosla design. If the city is wrapped in urgent issues of conservation of its grand architectural legacy, then since the 1990s its urban planners have also had to map time and space to accommodate shopping malls and multiplex cinemas. Alive to issues of preservation, Abu Jani Sandeep Khosla created four large 'Bombay City' wall hangings to support the cause of the conservation of Horniman Circle, a major city landmark (once known as the Bombay Green, it is the site for many cultural events, including the Kala Ghoda Arts Festival). The four panels, depicting historic city landmarks such as Victoria Terminus station, the Rajabahi clock tower, Mumbai University and Ballard estate, were auctioned. The Taj Group won the bid for three of the panels and these are prominently displayed in Taj hotels.

A greater public profile has also brought Abu Sandeep into an expansive circuit of charitable shows, museum exhibitions, television talk shows and awards. Their rise has coincided with globalism and an increasing influence and effect on the aesthetic appreciation of Indian art. In 1999, the Asia Society USA invited Abu and Sandeep to show their work in New York and Houston. In 2002, Selfridges in London invited them to participate in a month-long 'Bollywood' festival, where they recreated Dimple Kapadia's home, an aspect of crafted luxury born of fabulous invention. For the next two years they also retailed artifacts and home accessories at the store.

Cinema as inspiration and as outlet for work has also flourished in the pair's filmic associations, which cut across Hollywood and Bollywood. After Sophie Marceau and Judi Dench, Freida Pinto wore their clothes to all the red-carpet events around the London premiere of

(Below and centre) Abu and Sandeep receiving the National Award for Best Costume Design for the film Devdas *from the President of India, Abdul Kalam Azad, 2003.*

Slumdog Millionaire. Abu Sandeep clothes for cinema also gained enormous visibility with their costumes for Madhuri Dixit, Shah Rukh Khan and Jackie Shroff in the Sanjay Leela Bhansali film *Devdas*, for which they were awarded the prestigious National Award for Best Costume Design (2003).

With a return to the ramp in the last decade, Abu Sandeep have reaffirmed their design values in outstanding craftsmanship. In 2006, they were invited to present a twenty-year retrospective in the form of a highly feted fashion show at the FDCI India Fashion Week in New Delhi. Four years later they created the grand finale for the Pearl Couture week with the show 'Almost 24', at which they presented a number of lines from the span of their career. Also in 2010, among stellar Indians from the worlds of industry, entertainment and sport, including Ratan Tata, Amitabh Bachchan, A. R. Rahman and Sachin Tendulkar, Abu and Sandeep were honoured at the Asian Awards, when international designer Christian Louboutin presented them with the prize for Outstanding Achievement in Art and Design.

Within the factory at Ghanshyam Industrial Estate, the changes in contemporary India are also being registered. On different levels, in separate galas, chiffon is dyed and cut for the haveli of Parveen Bhabhi, which produces its careful and meticulous chikankari at Kakori. At an Abu Jani Sandeep Khosla factory in Goregaon, twelve men huddle around a single sari, embroidering an entire glittering Persian landscape in fine zardozi, while in a neighbouring workshop scores of machine workers spin out the newest Abu Sandeep diffusion line, marketed under the label Abu Sandeep.

The difference between haute couture and diffusion is that, while the former is one of a kind, diffusion runs into a series of three garments, not unlike limited edition objects. The diffusion line under the label Abu Sandeep is intended for the upwardly mobile, aspirational buyer and was launched in 2007. In the same year, the first Abu Sandeep store opened in Delhi. Their haute couture outlets also proliferated. In 2008, they moved from their store in Greater Kailash II to the Emporio Mall in New Delhi.

Diffusion engages the idea of Indo-Western design, marking the recognition of a new globalized India with a demographic overwhelmingly in favour of the young. The styling has become more democratic and broad-based: thus Mughal-designed appliqués replace intensive embroidery, and folk motifs, mirror work and machine embroidery make a vivid appearance. Diffusion also addresses the growing public curiosity about and interest in Abu Sandeep's work. Since their designs for *Devdas*, as well as their successful appearances in the television series *The First Ladies*, for which they interviewed India's prominent women, such as Nita Ambani, Gauri Khan, Padmini Devi of Jaipur and Usha Mittal, Abu and Sandeep have become the supreme Indian design luxury label. Yet even as they democratize and expand their markets, the reception to their brand becomes layered and complex. In recent times, their work has come to be regarded as a family heirloom, to be passed on from mother to daughter for perpetuity. It has entered into museum collections and become a slice of India's contemporary design history. At the same time, it has been imitated, copied and pirated.

Even after twenty-five years, the Abu Sandeep mystique continues to grow, beguiling the imagination with the promise of a self-perpetuating beauty. Against the vivid and frequently tumultuous success of the past, the preparation for the future draws on many aspects of their practice and a shifting vision. At its heart is the love for craft, for the generosity and the richness of tradition, and the desire to make it flourish and endure.

(Above) The most powerful women of India assembled for the first time for The First Ladies, *the television talk show hosted by Abu and Sandeep.*

(Opposite) Some of Abu Jani Sandeep Khosla's worldwide team.

SUNITA PITAMBER, WITH HER HUSBAND RANA RAJ KUMAR PITAMBER

"Sunita was a woman of substance, knowledge, style and grace. She was very well read;
knew her food, her art. She had a large heart. The cherry on top was her wit and sense of humour.
She hosted the greatest parties in her house, where one met the most accomplished
and the simplest people from around the world."

PARVIN MEHTA

*"P, as we lovingly called her, was the most delightful, positive
person. She lit up the room with happiness and laughter.
She was a very loyal friend and guided us through
some very trying times. We miss her greatly."*

BEGUM PARA

*"Begum had a larger-than-life personality. She was the first Indian
actress to be featured on the cover of Life magazine. She always
told Abu that she regretted not being born twenty years later
so that she could have an affair with him! She gifted us
our best friend and some of our best recipes."*

SHAMMI RABADI

*"Shammi is the oldest of our young friends. We believe that,
apart from our hard work, her prayers have been a large part
of our success. She continues to be our spiritual guide."*

EILEEN COYNE

*"Eileen is a large-hearted woman with an outsized laugh.
She is generous and opened her heart and house to us.
She is a creative jeweler and interior designer. She loves
our work and introduced our fashion to the West."*

Celebrating life with some friends.

"It's been a glorious journey. It seems as if it started only yesterday. There are no short cuts in life – we've worked hard – but we are blessed to have our friends and all the people who believe in Abu Jani Sandeep Khosla."

ABU SANDEEP

"Lotuses have been an eternal fascination for us. Here, three-dimensional embroidery appears on skin-coloured tulle, as if the lotuses are floating on a nude body."

"Beyond fashion."
PRINCESS LUCIANA PIGNATELLI

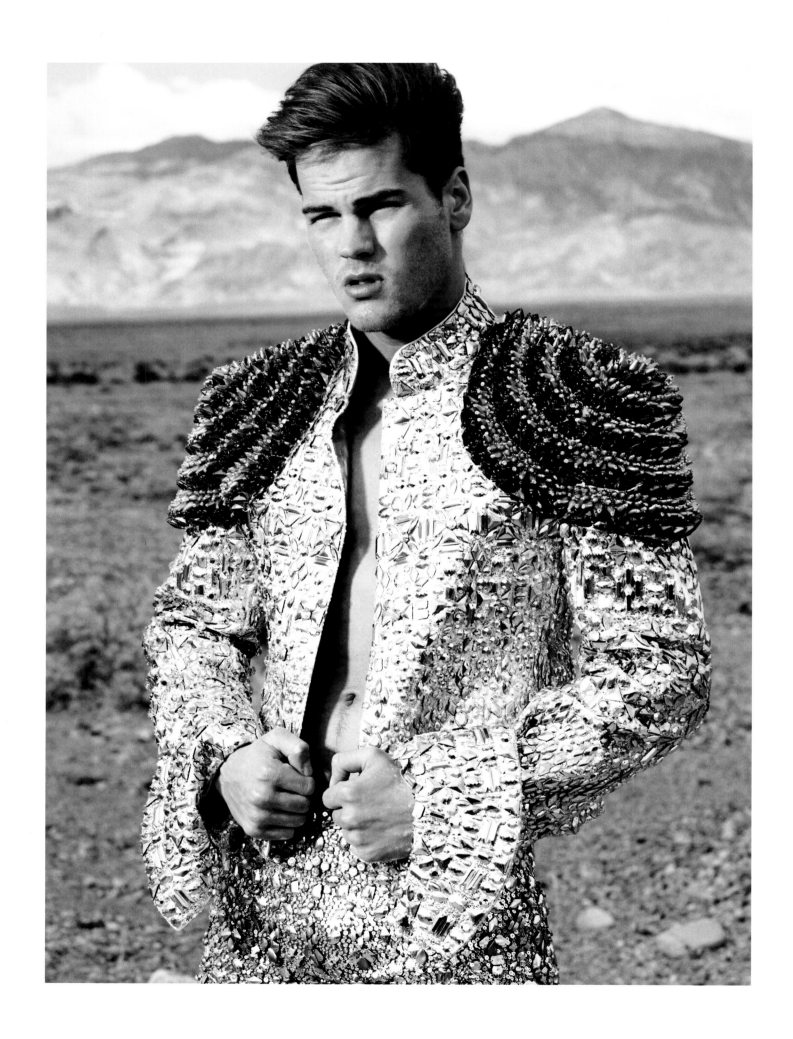

"Armoured shoulders and jewelled cuffs in gold-coloured gunmetal pieces sewn upright."

"A sheet of sequins layered with embroidery is the ultimate."

"*The embroidery on this kaftan
was inspired by the patterns in
a kaleidoscope.*"

63

EDGE OF DESIRE

"*Because we are untrained, nothing is impossible.*"

SANDEEP

"The name Abu Jani Sandeep
Khosla is reminiscent of old-
world charm and royalty."
SOCIETY MAGAZINE, 2006

71

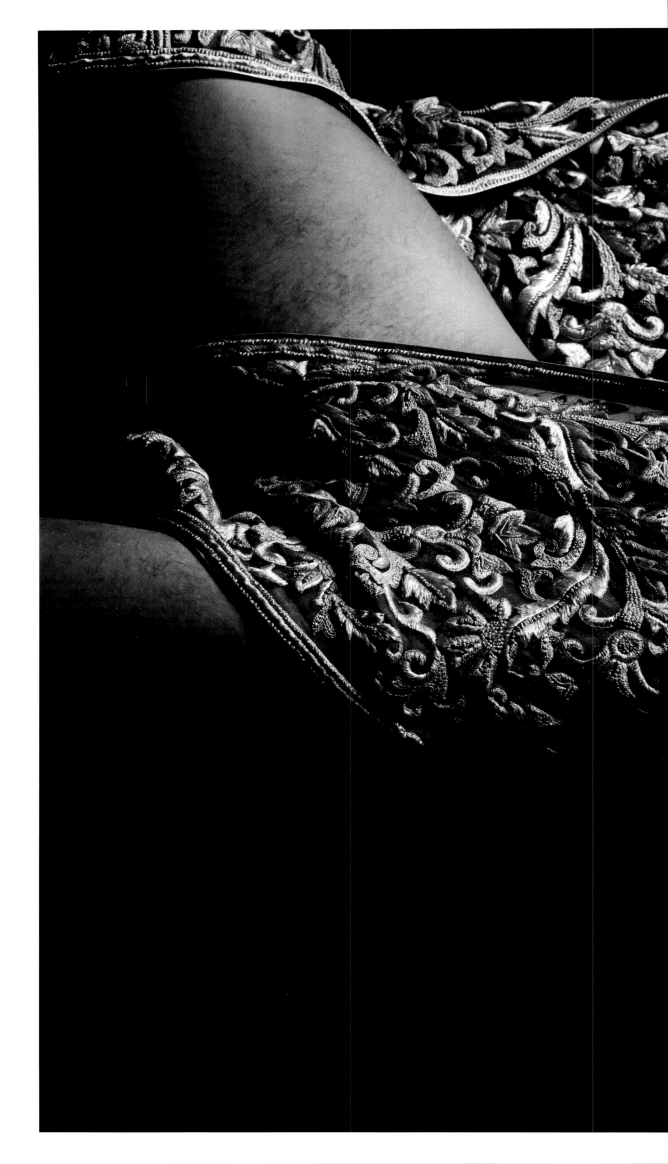

"These fine embroidery borders were inspired by Kashmiri paisley."

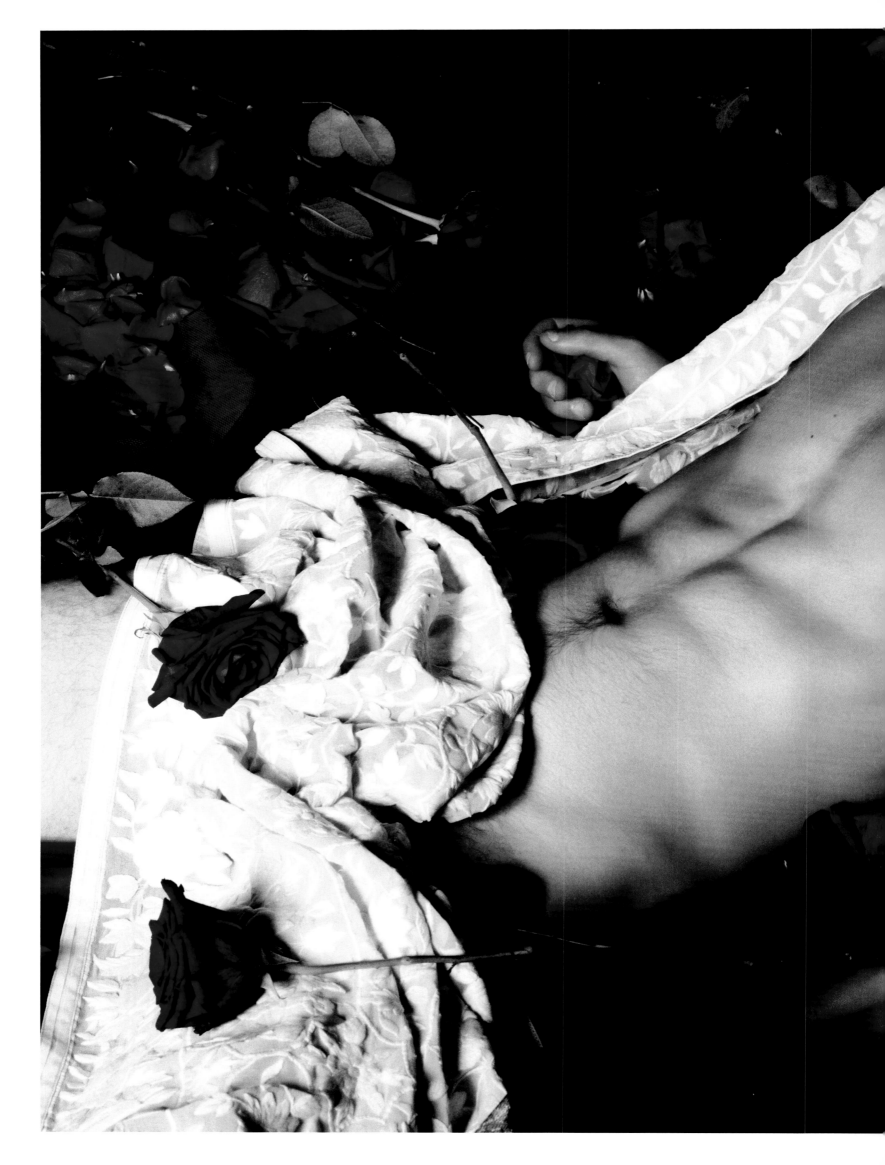

"A signature style that hinges on opulence…"

"We don't follow trends; we set them!"

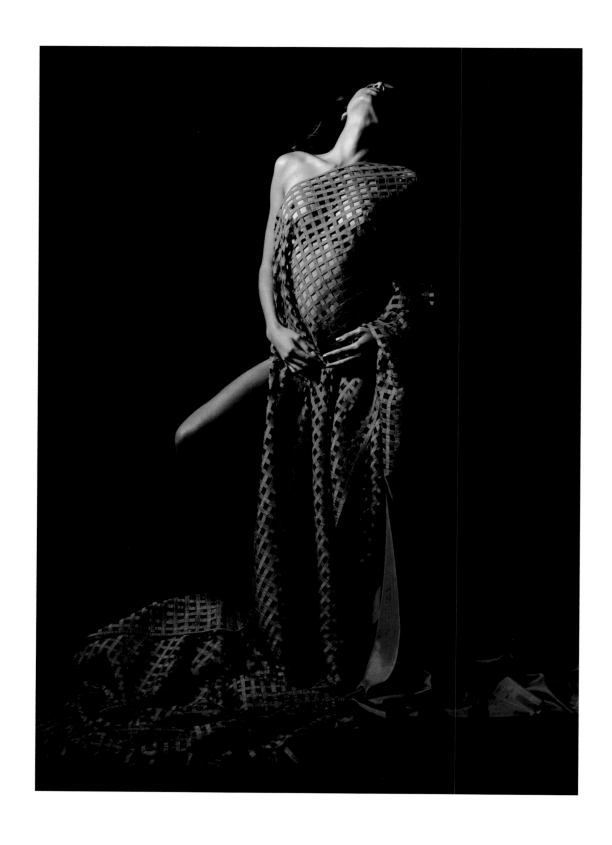

"The 'Rabadi' coat opposite is worn inside out to show the tailoring detail.
The inside of an Abu Jani Sandeep Khosla design is just as important as the outside."

"The dress opposite, with silk embroidery on georgette, was inspired by the Bharatpur bird sanctuary in Rajasthan."

FIVE AND A HALF YARDS

"*We are so indulgent in our thought that we are always trying to stay ahead of ourselves. Our intention is to be the most desired.*"

SANDEEP

"Truly beautiful work."
RAJMATA GAYATRI DEVI OF JAIPUR

"*A sari constructed in crushed raw silk: one of our earliest pieces.*"

THE SECRET GARDEN

*"We are as different as chalk and cheese,
but together we dream magical dreams,
and these translate into our clothes."*

ABU

"Abu Jani Sandeep Khosla designs are exquisite combinations of beautiful fabrics and embroidery techniques of the East, adding mystery and excitement to both day and evening wear."
LINDY HEMMING

"More is more. Metres and metres
of multipanelled, multicoloured
silk georgette…"

"This collection, using silk thread embroidery and mirror work, was inspired by the colours of Rajasthan."

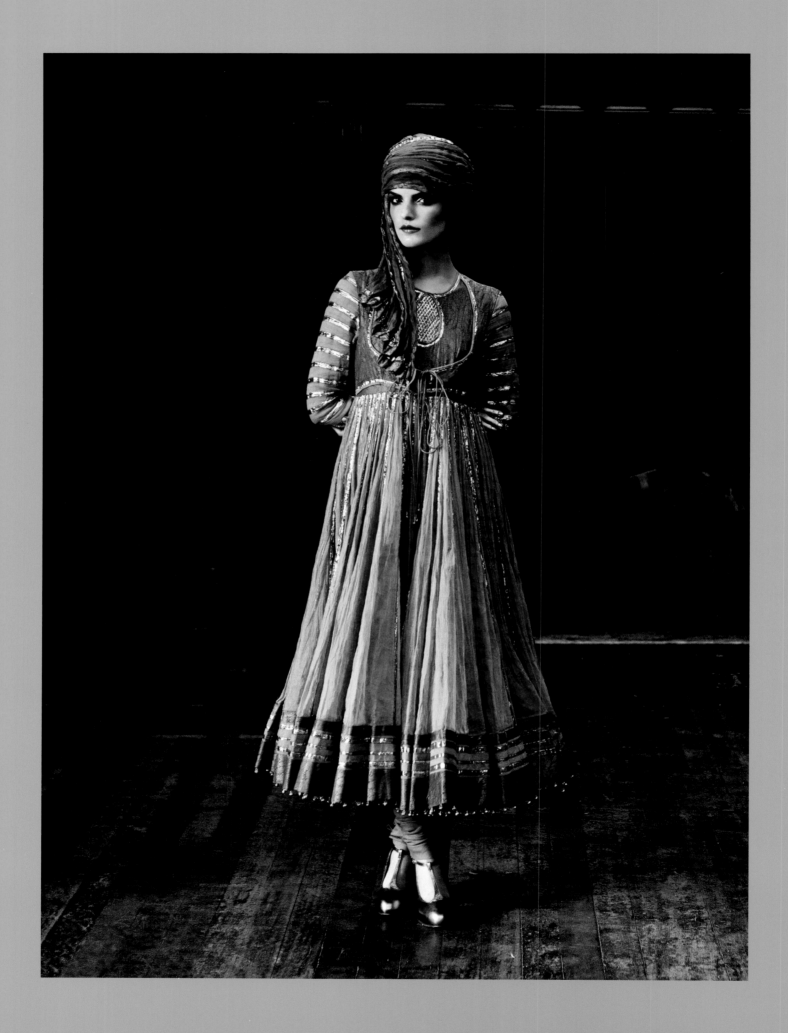

"Our clothes have a classic timelessness, an old-world charm. When you buy our clothes, you buy a little memory of India, of our history, our culture, our colours."

ABU SANDEEP

"*Abu and Sandeep are true artists, creating exquisite heirlooms.*"
JAYA BACHCHAN

"Dropping peacock feathers in multicoloured metallic sequins…"

"*The embroidery pattern above was inspired by the traditional Balinese form of movement in design.*"

*"An Abu Sandeep ensemble can take you to any party in the world
and you will shine among the world's best dressed women."*
SATURDAY TIMES, 1998

141

A VOYAGE INTO THE PAST

"*We believe in creating the most flamboyant, unashamedly extravagant outfits; in presenting a totally glamorous version of life for people who have forgotten how to dream.*"

SANDEEP

"Once we started our crushed line we wanted to experiment further, so we took yards of gold tissue and ruched it with embroidery stitches to make the ultimate long flared coat."

"Our trendsetting oversized mojaris, with their exaggerated soles, were custom-made and embroidered in zardozi. They are worn with Tibetan brocade trousers and a gold bead sherwani lined in brocade."

"Opposite is our first constructed sari drape, worn with dhoti trousers and a brocade jacket
with shoulder pads and puffed sleeves, from our debut Mata Hari collection in the late 1980s."

"Opposite are satin silk dresses with resham embroidery, inspired by dancing dolls."

"East meets West: a marriage of delicate resham embroidery with a dramatic sequinned hood."

"An early 'Architectural' coat, fully quilted, with three-dimensional silk thread embroidery, inspired by the ruins of Purana Qila, the historic old fort in New Delhi."

*"A black silk kaftan with a finely embroidered necklace of
miniature paintings framed by glass beads and zardozi embroidery."*

*"A 'Bedouin' coat, with embroidery on gold brocade,
inspired by the suzanis of Central Asia."*

173

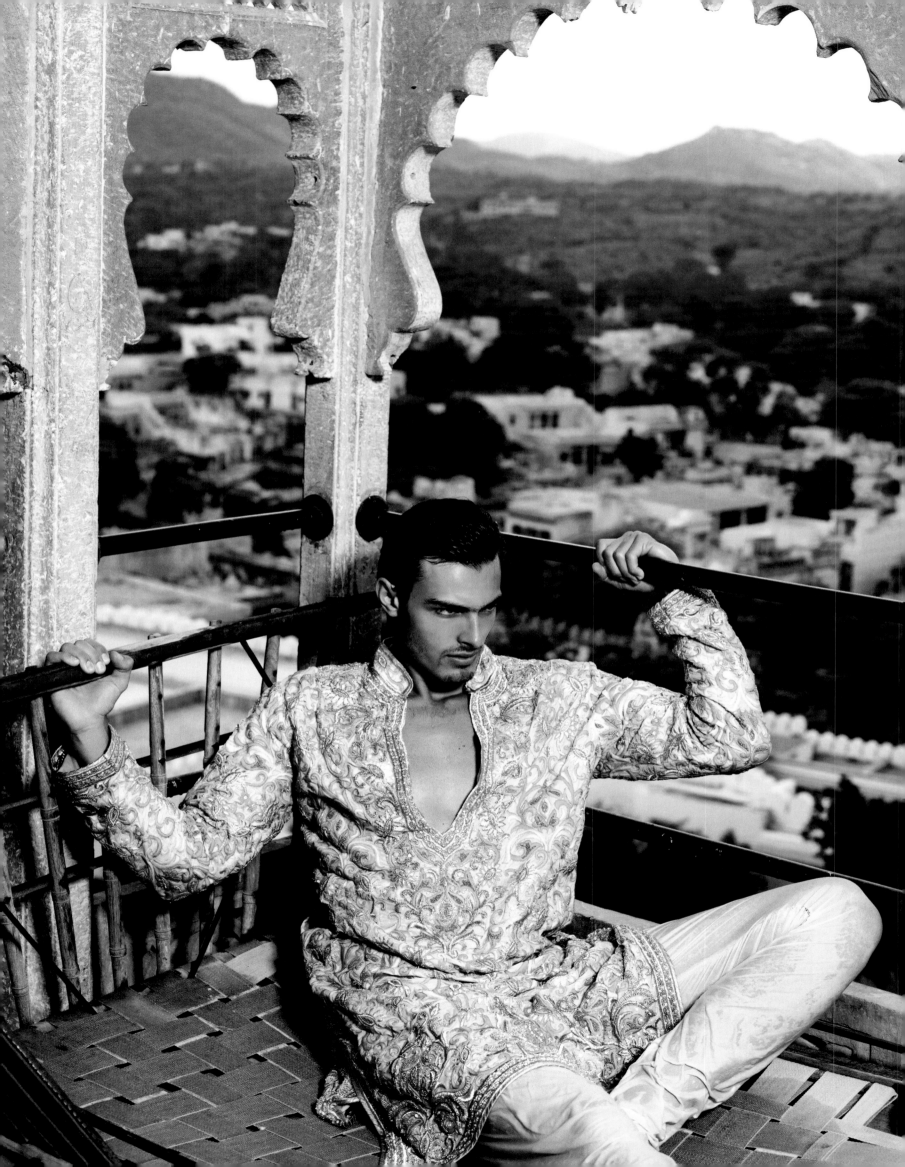

"*We like to do things in a lavish yet elegant manner.*
That's just how our style is – a celebration of life."

ABU

"*To be good enough is not good enough,*
a perfectionist once said. It's a dictum that
comes to mind when one tries to describe
the art of Abu Jani and Sandeep Khosla.
Their inspiration has always been the art
and craft of the Orient, but the method of
their expression belongs to the Occident."
SUNITA PITAMBER

"Abu Jani Sandeep Khosla outfits are
treated as family heirlooms, to be cherished,
worn at special occasions and handed
down from generation to generation."
SUNDAY MID DAY, 1995

THE ROYAL PARADE

"*Everything in our life has to please our aesthetic. It is never minimal. At the same time it does not follow any discipline.*"

ABU

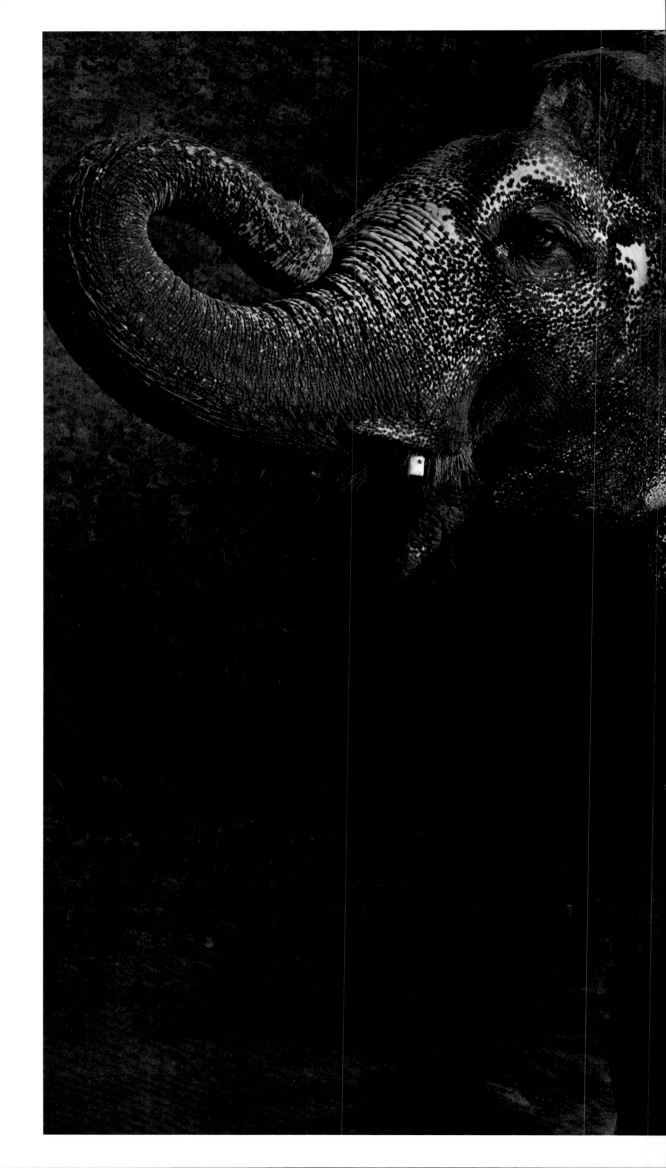

*"Abu Jani Sandeep Khosla broke
the mindset that white was an
inauspicious colour."*
THE HINDU, 2001

"The Chikan Collection defies
classification. It is not just an
array of ensemble, not a mere
fashion statement, not just
something to wear this summer.
It is something everyone craves for."

THE ASIAN AGE, 1997

"*Our clothes are for women who have led a life under the arc-lights. We believe that our clothes can enhance anyone's inner self.*"

SANDEEP

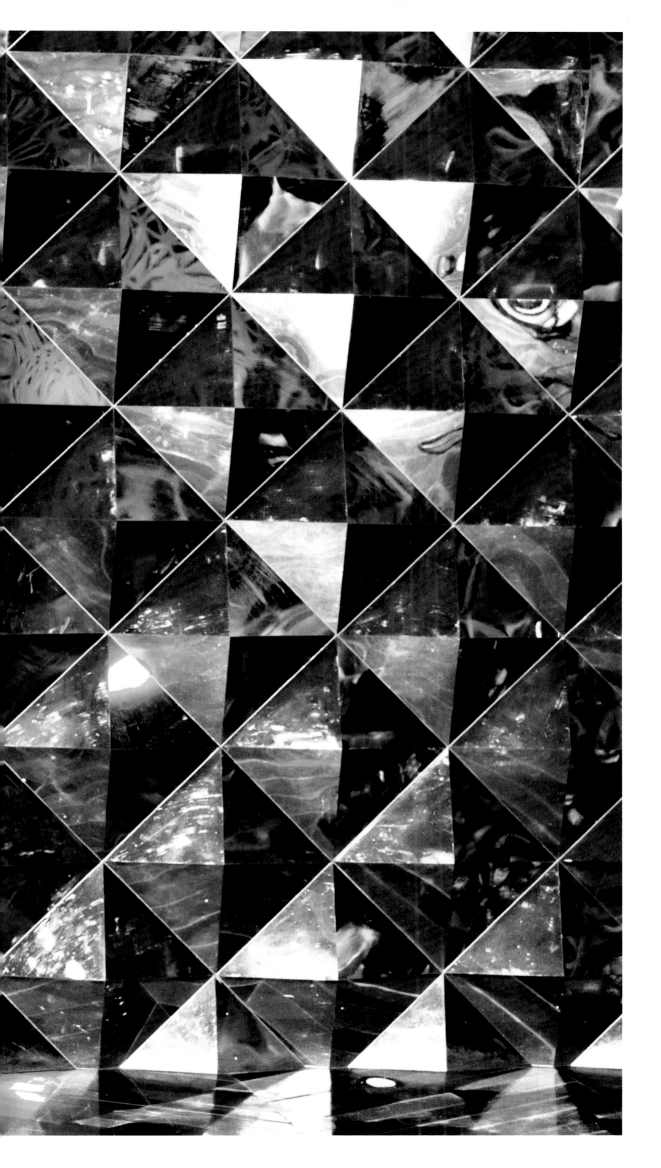

"A dress made with stones, sequins and individually embroidered silk petals in gold organza, joined to form three-dimensional roses that cover skin-coloured net."

"Abu Jani Sandeep Khosla's insane love for embroidery leads them to produce exquisite works of art, ostensibly for wearing, but perfect enough to drape on your walls like a painting."
THE SUNDAY OBSERVER, 1998

"A gold and silver bead tasselled skirt and a pair of velvet trousers studded with Swarovski crystals."

USHA MITTAL *wears Lace Floral for Abu Jani Sandeep Khosla*
"Greater than the power of wealth is the power family... Usha Mittal understands this and holds the emotional
and pragmatic reins of a global empire. She blends a value system beautifully alongside corporate power." ABU SANDEEP

"*Our strongest relationships have come through our work.*"

ABU SANDEEP

It has been almost fifteen years since I first came to know Abu Jani and Sandeep Khosla. From the
very beginning I was struck by their creativity, commitment and keen sense of detail. Since then,
I have always been able to count on them for exceptional designs, some of which were for the most
memorable events of my family life, the weddings of our children Aditya to Megha, and Vanisha to Amit.
Over these years, it has been a pleasure to see Abu and Sandeep go from strength to strength
in the world of fashion as well as other forms of design. They must be applauded for an immense
contribution in taking fashion design to the level of art by integrating traditional Indian and modern
styles in a truly unique manner. The prominence that they enjoy today in India and globally is
a testament to their high calibre and dedication.
This book is a celebration of Abu and Sandeep's achievements, of which I am sure there will be
many more to come. I do hope that you enjoy reading about these two wonderfully talented
individuals, for whom design is their calling.

Usha Mittal

USHA MITTAL

NITA AMBANI AND HER DAUGHTER ISHA *wear Chikan (opposite) and Bali Gota (above) for Abu Jani Sandeep Khosla*
"She may be at the helm of a corporate empire, but there is much more to Nita Ambani
than her global power... A humanitarian and a woman of tremendous substance,
she is the silent and stoic strength of her family." ABU SANDEEP

DIMPLE KAPADIA *ACTRESS wears Chikan for Abu Jani Sandeep Khosla*

THE SUPERSTARS

"*They own the limelight. They are the demi-gods of celluloid. Iconic, inspirational, and always a part of our home and fashion house...*"

ABU SANDEEP

DIMPLE KAPADIA *wears Khadi Zardozi for Abu Jani Sandeep Khosla*
"Dimple Kapadia has been our muse for almost twenty-five years. Her sheer beauty leaves us spellbound. With her beauty comes a naïve and clean heart, which leaves her incapable of doing any harm. This makes her even more beautiful. She always strives to give 1000% to every 1% that is given to her."
ABU SANDEEP

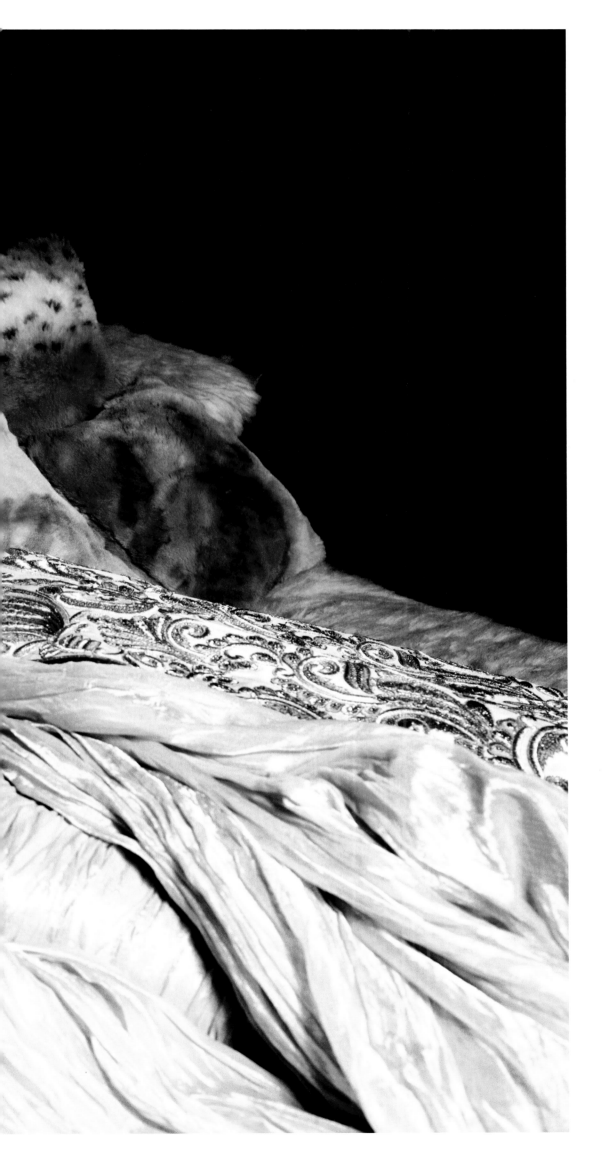

AMITABH BACHCHAN *ACTOR wears*
Abaan for Abu Jani Sandeep Khosla
"There are those whose achievements
are unparalleled; there are those whose
legendary body of work constantly
overwhelms us; there are those whose
imprints are all over global archives...
All that and more still does not quantify
the magnitude of Amitabh Bachchan.
We are blessed to have him in our
life. He is, and always will be, our
inspiration." ABU SANDEEP

DAME JUDI DENCH *ACTRESS*
wears Chikan [White] (above) and Vasli [Black] (opposite)
"It has been an honour and a privilege to have the trust of an actor of world renown.
Dame Judi Dench has always given us carte blanche to dress her for important red-carpet events.
She brings regal grace to our outfits, and we treasure our association with her." ABU SANDEEP

(*Opposite*) DIMPLE KAPADIA AND HER DAUGHTERS TWINKLE KHANNA AND RINKE SARAN *ACTRESSES*
wear Zardozi for Abu Jani Sandeep Khosla

(*Above*) NAOMIKA SARAN *wears Chikan Zardozi for Abu Jani Sandeep Khosla*
"Three generations of stunning beauty and large hearts...
We are blessed to have them as a part of our family." ABU SANDEEP

(Above and opposite) SALMAN KHAN *ACTOR*
wears Zardozi for Abu Jani Sandeep Khosla
**"He takes superstardom to an incomprehensible level. His connection to millions
of people across the world is unparalleled. Camera-easy, unapologetic and
an active humanitarian, Salman Khan is a movie Mughal."** ABU SANDEEP

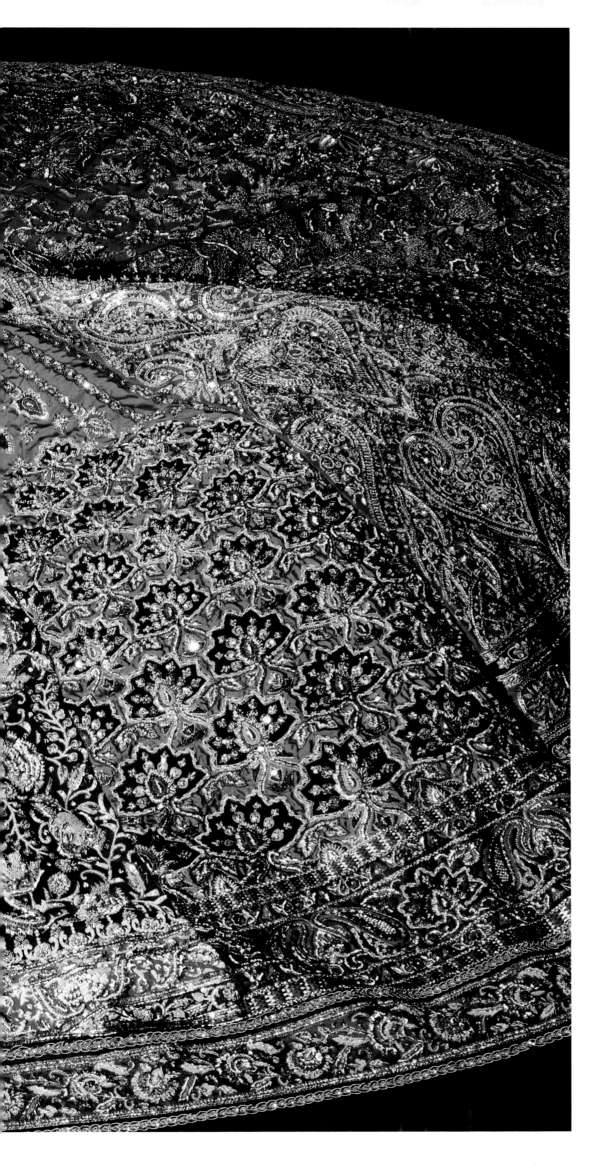

SHWETA NANDA *STYLE ICON* wears
Zardozi for Abu Jani Sandeep Khosla
"A glorious chip off a legendary block.
A daughter that is every father's pride.
A mother that daughters and sons dream of.
A home-maker, and our family forever.
Shweta Bachchan Nanda ... our soul
daughter in every lifetime." ABU SANDEEP

235

(Opposite) SONALI BENDRE ACTRESS *wears Mirror Work for Abu Jani Sandeep Khosla*
"Elegance, poise and carriage best classify the magic of Sonali Bendre." ABU SANDEEP

(Above) SUSSANNE ROSHAN INTERIOR DESIGNER *wears Shabb for Abu Jani Sandeep Khosla*
**"Great lineage, superstar arm candy and now an aesthetic entrepreneur,
Sussanne Roshan stands tall."** ABU SANDEEP

(Above and opposite) HRITHIK ROSHAN *ACTOR wears Stone for Abu Jani Sandeep Khosla*
**"Spiritual and sexy, Hrithik Roshan defines what Greek gods stood for.
But being gorgeous is just one of his assets. He is one of the best actors
in Indian cinema and has the talent to conquer the world."** ABU SANDEEP

SHWETA NANDA *wears Sonar (opposite) and Dhaka (above) for Abu Jani Sandeep Khosla*

(Above) JAYA BACHCHAN AND HER DAUGHTER SHWETA NANDA
wear Gota Borders for Abu Jani Sandeep Khosla

(Opposite) AMRITA SINGH AND HER DAUGHTER SARA ALI KHAN
wear Rabadi for Abu Jani Sandeep Khosla
"Amrita Singh, who we lovingly call Dingi, is an actress par excellence. She is a great friend,
with tremendous spontaneous wit. Her intelligence and curiosity are in a class of their own,
as are her determination and strength. She has been a tremendous support to us." ABU SANDEEP

(Above and opposite) TABU ACTRESS *wears Chikan for Abu Jani Sandeep Khosla*
"Eyes that do what words can't. Expressions that convey what thoughts can't.
Tabu was born to communicate on celluloid. She shuns glamour but has always
embraced our embellished arms. A personal favourite for her soul connect." ABU SANDEEP

(Left and above) SHAH RUKH KHAN AND HIS WIFE GAURI
wear Lace for Abu Jani Sandeep Khosla
**"Rarely do you meet couples who get it all right. She is the ultimate
glamour girl; he is an enviable superstar. She is exotic ... and he makes
unconventional look sexier than ever. Together they leave an indelible
impression wherever they go. Shah Rukh and Gauri are the
aspirational couple and live the dream."** ABU SANDEEP

247

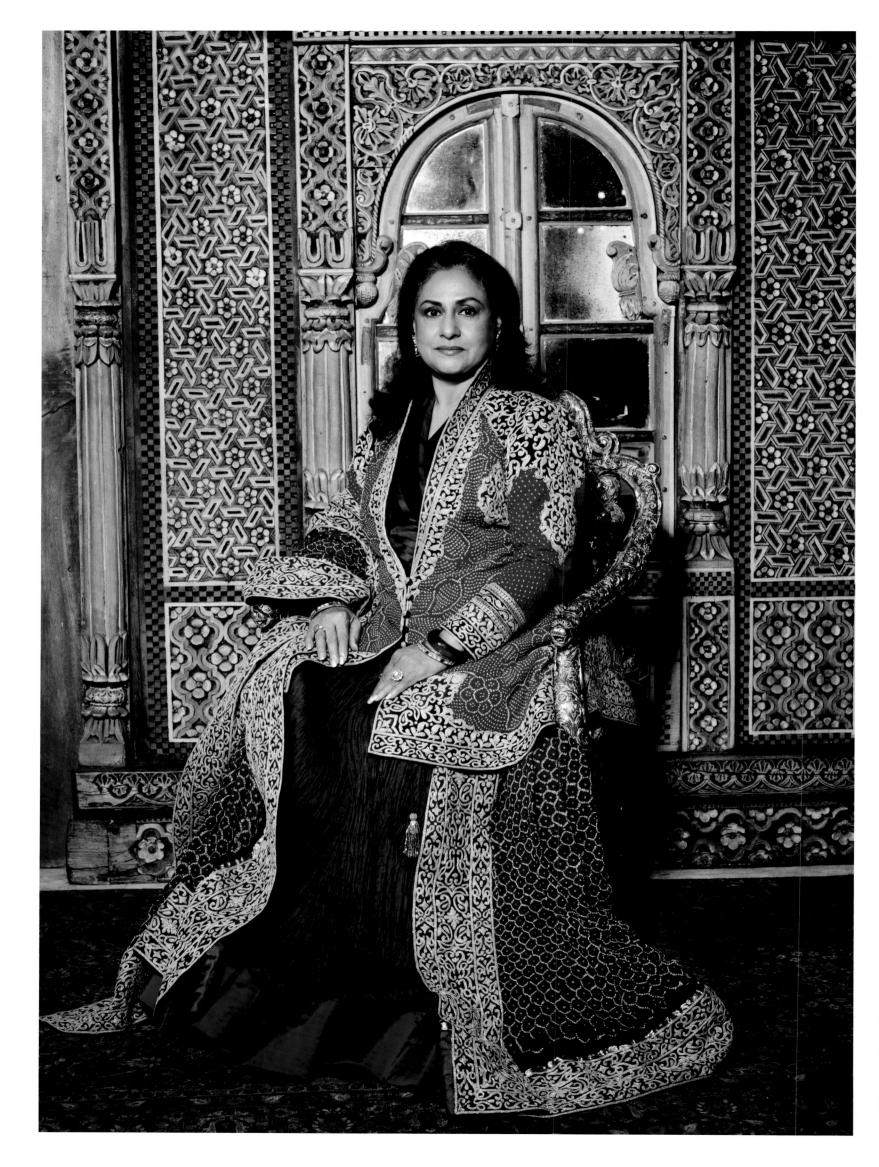

JAYA BACHCHAN *wears Marodi for Abu Jani Sandeep Khosla*
"Jaya has been our biggest supporter and has believed in us. Not one to be impulsive, she takes her time, but, once she starts believing, nothing can change or deter that belief. She has a fine eye for spotting talent, and a keen interest for detail. She is very literate, like her father, who was an accomplished writer. She has supported us through a lot of our hard times and good times emotionally. She has been our strength, and continues to be so." ABU SANDEEP

Antique bakhia booti, embellished with a phanda stitch.

"Chikan is an art form that should be done at leisure.
It is beautiful, it is conventional, it is classic.
And so it is forever."

ABU SANDEEP

Men's kurta (back view), with a bakhia paan (leaf) motif on a diagonal bakhia and keel jaal (trellis) (see also p. 262).

white on white

Bakhia and murri-stitch paan, with borders of bakhia javas (leaves).

Since Anarkali and Sahibjaan, the historic courtesans of Delhi and Awadh, had already been nominated as beacons of inspiration for Abu and Sandeep, a greater investigation on their part into the arts of decoration was inevitable. The pair became particularly interested in India's fabled embroidery skills. This interest was more unusual than it first appears. The documentation and revival of the craft movement in India was mainly centred around the sari and its numerous weaves. These weaves were revived, documented and revisited in the research of many textile historians, the narrative hinging around the craft of weaving and its museumization, revival and uses. However, as Abu notes, 'embroidery never got that importance'.

In the evanescent trail of Sahibjaan, Abu and Sandeep turned to Lucknow, with its rich if gently decaying history. Situated along the vast swathe of the Gangetic plane of northern India, Lucknow, or the medieval state of Awadh, has had a cultural history that is distinct from the vast overarching Mughal influence on the north. A Shia kingdom with its own distinct culinary style, ornamental architecture, courtly manners and style of dress, Lucknow reached the zenith of 'ada' (an Urdu term connoting traditions, etiquette and manners) during the British era. Abdul Halim Sharar, journalist and chronicler of nineteenth-century Lucknow under Nawab Wajid Ali Shah, writes of female fashion of the time that chikan was much loved in the Nawab's court, and that the angarkha tunic and the doshala scarf were widely used by the royal court as gifts: 'Both these garments came to Lucknow from Delhi, but the scarves were more often seen in Lucknow. In the hot weather, embroidered muslin scarves were worn and these were part of the dress of all elegant people. They covered their heads with topis (caps) of chikan work, their bodies with angarkhas, their legs with wide pyjamas, and over their shoulders they draped scarves of light muslin or tulle. This was the accepted fashion of the upper classes and elegant people in Lucknow.'

'Glistening, white and shining': the chikan narrative in Abu Jani Sandeep Khosla's history appears as a series of happy unfoldings and bold enterprises. In its beauty, this fabric would have sat comfortably on any of the residents of Wajid Ali Shah's fabled palace along the Gomti river. By the early 1990s, Abu and Sandeep had worked inventively on zardozi, Gujarati mirror work, resham (silk thread) embroidery and crushed fabric. They were ready for an infusion of new energy. In 1991, Sandeep heard of his cousin Sita Sondhi and her friend Shahnaaz Kidwai's modest and highly individualized revival of chikankari in Lucknow. Members of old aristocratic Lucknow families, Sita and Shahnaaz found that chikankari was in an abysmal state. The decline was already entrenched when the women determined to see if they could reverse it. 'What was available in 1991 was the worst quality of shadow work that was being sold in the name of chikan,' says Shahnaaz. 'Traditional patronage had also become impoverished in the middle of the twentieth century, and chikan nearly disappeared. The art of chikankari shifted from male embroiderers to almost exclusively female embroiderers, and the work slipped from mahin (fine) to mota (thick). Fortunately, by then a pioneer organization – SEWA, the Self-Employed Women's Association – had started work among chikan workers, trying to empower them and to bypass the middleman. The government also had a department providing a similar service.' In the main, crude heavy stitches on nylon saris in lurid pastels, children's frocks and tableware were strung out for streetside display in Lucknow's Hazratganj and Aminabad markets: Sita and Shahnaaz's efforts to push for a better quality of embroidery on their own clothes met with slow but perceptible success. They began to make clothes for themselves and for their friends. It was at this juncture that Sandeep heard of their work and took the Shatabdi express train to Lucknow.

*(Above and opposite below) Kaftan, with
an antique phanda-stitch kairi (raw
mango) motif, with bakhia and murri
bakhia-stitch borders.*

To anyone familiar with the use of the craft in the Lucknow bazaars, and with the Abu Jani Sandeep Khosla line of utter sophistication, the transformation seems magical. When scouring the bazaars of old Lucknow, Sandeep and Abu went to the Chowk area – a place replete with eighteenth- and nineteenth-century architecture with Mughal associations. There, in an 11 x 5-foot space, the septuagenarian Mohammed Ali showed them hundreds of disused chikan blocks, once used by master embroiderers.

Chikankari is believed to have been revived and developed as a cottage industry by Noor Jahan, Empress of India and a great aesthete. The craft's fortunes ebbed and flowed with history and patronage. The British occupancy of Lucknow, Wajid Ali Shah's exile to Matia Burj and the Partition of India, when the cream of Lucknow's Muslim aristocracy left for Pakistan, all dented the craft. Nevertheless it remained the preferred artform of the Lucknow aristocracy. Traditionally embroidered with white on white, chikan is associated with the giving of gifts. Thus, every year, together with mangoes from the fragrant orchards of Malihabad, new chikan kurtas would be presented to sons-in-law, sons, husbands and nephews.

In 1991, examining block prints in the evening light filtering through Mohammed Ali's tiny room, and doodling around the designs, Abu reached the apex of the chain of chikankari – creative block maker. 'I had never done any printing,' he says, 'but the purity of chikan challenged me. It was a chance to break all the rules.' From this fortuitous encounter it was another two years of stubborn experimentation before the first garments were ready. 'We are so indulgent in our thought that we are always trying to stay ahead of ourselves. Our intention is to be the most desired,' says Sandeep. He and Abu chose chiffon as their material. The long, interdependent chain of craftspeople, including Sita and Shahnaaz, were used to fine muslin and cotton, and they resisted. The main challenge was: how could this delicate material endure the tough washing processes necessary without becoming damaged? 'The chikan wash,' confirm Abu and Sandeep, 'is extremely harsh on fabric.' The hurdles were manifold. Chikan designs, which are printed with gum and indigo, are traditionally washed in the waters of Lucknow's river Gomti. 'Dhobis [washermen] let the river flow through the garment till it slowly dissolves and draws the gum and indigo away. Only then can any other cleaning process take place.' Another hurdle was obtaining kachha taaga, or cotton thread; most embroiderers have shifted to polyester thread since it is easier to wash and dye. Fortunately, the slew of constraints did not dim the pair's conviction.

Fourteen kilometres outside the city stands Kakori, the greatest centre of the naat genre of poetry, and the abode of the Kakorvi Shaikh community. Here, at the haveli of Parveen Abbasi, fondly known as Parveen Bhabhi, Abu Jani Sandeep Khosla initiated a quiet revolution in chikan. The tradition of chikankari in Kakori is reflected in the antiquity of some of the intricately carved wooden blocks used there for printing the chikan patterns.

The carved wooden block is at the fountainhead of chikan. It is stamped on the cloth and the design is then carefully embroidered over. The block designer is considered the true artist of the form, and this is where Abu Sandeep's intervention came in. In a conventional design, two or three blocks are normally used. Abu Sandeep have used as many as twenty-five in a garment, rendering it a complex web of forms and motifs.

When, after years of expensive trial and error, the first high-fashion garments of elaborate and highly detailed chikan work were displayed, they revealed embroidery in gentle relief covering the expansive fabric, at once delicate and highly feminine. During the British period, long sweeping pyjamas had been forbidden as an indulgence; now the fabric swayed, moved and draped to a pre-modern rhythm of luxurious excess.

(Above) Sari, with antique bakhia surahi jaal (flowered trellis) motifs and multiple borders.

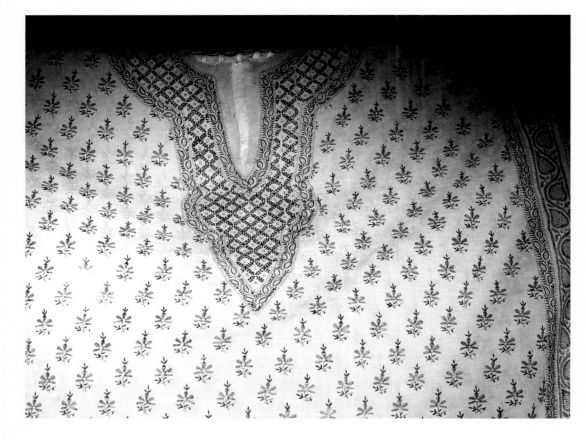

(Below) Chikan jaal and other motifs are inspired by local Indian architecture.

(Centre) A selection of blocks used by Abu Sandeep.

(Bottom) An architectural detail of fish motifs on an arch, typical of Lucknow. Wajid Ali Shah, Nawab of Lucknow, was very fond of fish, so the motif is found on old buildings throughout the city.

(Right) Embroidery being carried out after the fabric has been printed. Each stitch is done by a different woman. Since every garment contains several stitches, it is worked on by many women. Here, a group of workers is seen carrying out individual stitches on a single garment.

(Opposite above) The typical printing set-up for chikan. The blocks are dipped in a mixture of gum and indigo, then printed on the fabric.

(Opposite below) Samples of embroidery stitching on printed patterns.

Abu Sandeep revealed their chikan line at a show in Delhi's Oberoi Hotel, which was attended by, among others, Sonia Gandhi and Rajmata Gayatri Devi, Maharani Padmini of Jaipur, with her daughter Diya. What immediately became clear was that in chikan Abu Sandeep had found a perennial fashion. The combination of a feudal craft revival with haute couture had been successfully achieved. The beauty of the fabrics was deeply persuasive: it allowed brides to wear white and middle-aged women to luxuriate in yards and yards of white chiffon with floral and geometric motifs. Abu Sandeep led chikan to appear mature, bold and convincing. Translated onto organza, chiffon, georgettes and silk, the chikan work was the culmination of a fantasy, a quest to realize what had not previously existed. 'Everything in our life has to please our aesthetic,' says Sandeep. 'It is never minimal. At the same time it does not follow any discipline.'

To examine an Abu Jani Sandeep Khosla chikan garment is to identify elements of conventional embroidery and chikan stitches such as the 'jaal', which is floral and comprises flowers, leaves and stems as well as the paisley motif. There is the six-thread pechni, one of the major stitches in chikan; murri, used to create leaves or petals; and phanda, which, as its name suggests, creates a knot, one of the best known stitches in chikan. The floral element is offset by geometric trellises, which bear comparison with Mughal architecture and monuments. Chikan boasts Turkish and Persian influences, not unlike Kashmiri carpets. Interestingly, the stark white of chikan has been modified further with a tea dye that gives the garments a warmer tone. Such austere and pure shades were ideal for the city of Mumbai, with its warm climate and its glut of Bollywood chromatic excess, shine and glitter. To chikan Abu Sandeep have added embellishments, such as crystal, zardozi and sequins, building up layers in low relief, or even with a three-dimensional effect, to evoke texture and light.

The success of the chikan line was witnessed at a show in Roosevelt House in New Delhi, residence of Frank Wisner, the US ambassador. Abu Sandeep dedicated the show to a charity, Butterflies. Titled 'Abu Jani Sandeep Khosla Overture', the show presented fashion in the form of theatre against the constructed backdrop of the historic Purana Qila. At the event they introduced a young and relatively unknown Shankar Mahadevan, now world-famous as a singer and composer. To celebrate and mark the line, they also brought out a book on chikan to document its stitches and celebrate its pristine beauty.

(Right) Sita Sondhi, Sandeep's aunt, and her friend Shahnaaz Kidwai, who helped Abu and Sandeep establish their chikan embroidery centre in Lucknow.

(Below) Garments at the dhobi ghat (washerman's area) on the banks of the river Gomti.

(Bottom) The flower market in Lucknow. Flowers can be seen in many chikan motifs.

(Opposite) A long, multipanelled dress with an assortment of chikan patterns that form a 'calendar' of blocks.

In the last twenty-five years, chikan has flourished, and Abu and Sandeep have become its unparalleled exponents and interpreters. Workshops have sprung up in and around the village of Kakori. About seventy-five stitches have been revived from this medieval craft, and women embroiderers have prospered. Abu speaks of the creative process as demanding, even tortuous: each design has to be superior to the last. 'A lot of my translations I am satisfied with, but I am very self-critical before a design is realized. I also tear and throw away so much work. In my mind there is a debate, an argument, to realize something, but I am never confident, never satisfied.' Each year Abu and Sandeep spend a week in Lucknow, with Sita and Shahnaaz, dipping into the city's slow rhythms of culinary delights, visits to Sufi shrines, music and the pleasure of creating their own design blocks. 'It challenges us to decide how we are going to print.' Abu Sandeep have reinterpreted chikan: the block meant for one stitch may be used for another in unexpected permutations. Chikan has been adapted to garments as diverse as ghagras for women and sherwanis for men, and Western-style jackets and women's trousers.

Judi Dench is one of their most visible stars. When filming on *The World is Not Enough*, she discovered that the film's stylist, Lindy Hemming, had bought their clothes for her co-star Sophie Marceau. Abu Sandeep's clothes thus gained high visibility in a James Bond film. Hemming herself wore their clothes to the Academy Awards, when she won for Best Costume Design for Mike Leigh's *Topsy-Turvy*. Judi Dench visited their store and befriended them, and has worn the Abu Jani Sandeep Khosla chikan line for six Bafta and Oscar award ceremonies. She describes their clothes as 'the most exquisitely feminine clothes I have ever worn'.

Murri-stitch jaali, featuring a full lotus, with bakhia, phanda and jaali stitches.

Men's kurta (front view) with a phanda lotus border and a jaali of phanda phool stitches forming a trellis (see also p. 252).

Long kurta with an antique phanda-stitch paan, surrounded by hatkatee stitches.

Large dupatta showing various chikan stitches, including bakhia phool chameli, chakalia, bakhia kairi, murri, jaal and lotus, with a phanda bail (trellis).

Unconventionally structured dress, resulting from Abu and Sandeep 'playing' with blocks and not adhering to rules. Starting with multiple borders that sandwich a block normally used on the body of a garment and not on the border, pyramids are formed using small blocks that climb to the top of the garment. Small filler blocks adorn the upward moving lines.

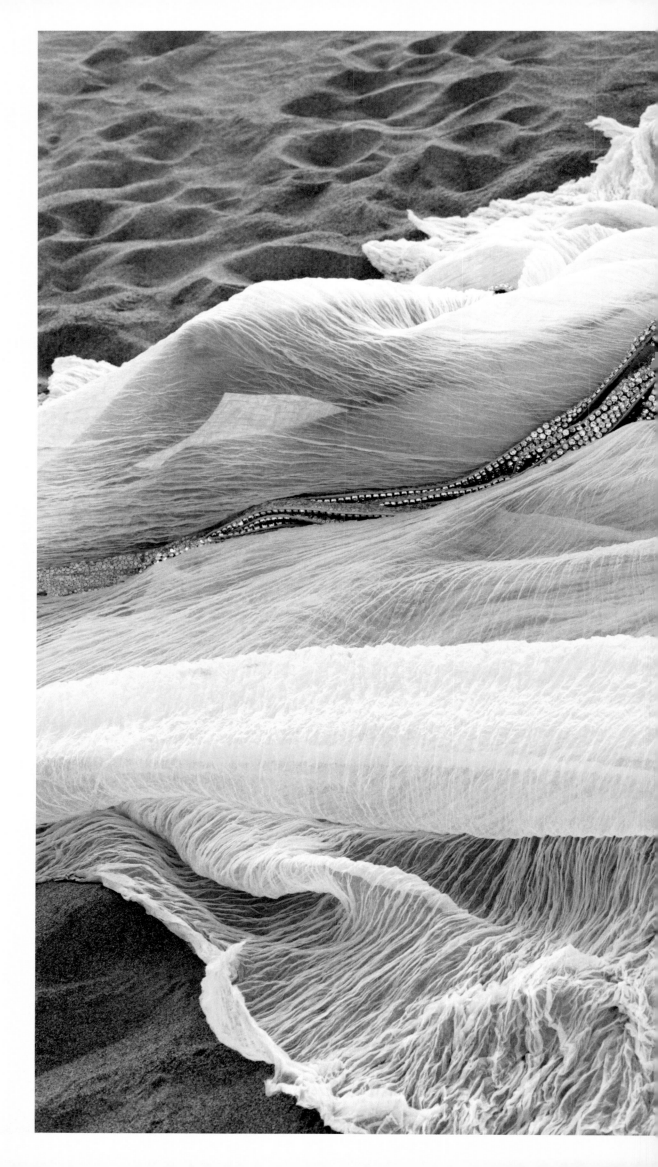

Fantasy garment, with heavy crystal chains, showcasing Abu and Sandeep's longstanding love of crush, white and crystals.

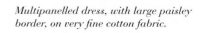

Multipanelled dress, with large paisley border, on very fine cotton fabric.

Antique phanda-stitch balls with a paan motif.

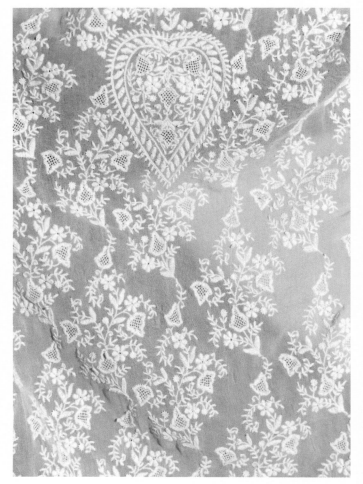

Murri-stitch paan with bakhia-stitch flower motifs.

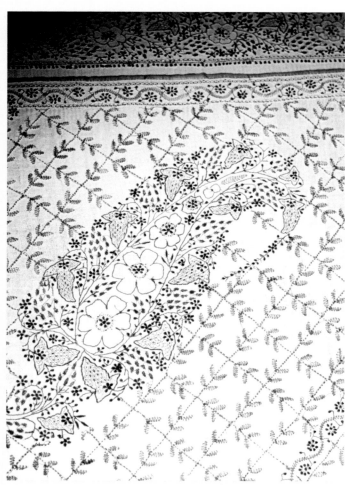

Antique phanda kairi and bakhia trellis.

Mughal booti with old bakhia-stitch trellis.

Various examples of Abu Sandeep's chikan work, many using motifs and stitches of historic heritage, including antiques of over a century in age. Each sample includes a wide variety of stitches, with the most notable cited.

Old phanda-stitch border and block of four flowers.

Murri and phanda-stitch moon earring and hatkatee-stitch crescents.

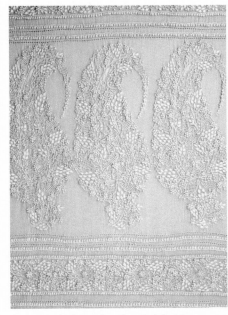

Border with old bakhia stitches.

Antique phanda-stitch kairi with phanda-stitch borders.

Antique bakhia-stitch booti embellished with ghumer stitches.

Old phanda-stitch jaal.

Old phanda block with hatkatee-stitch stems.

Bijli-stitch bootis with assorted borders.

273

Mirror work with zardozi on shaded silk georgette.

THE GOLDEN THREAD

*"Our love for embroidery continues undimmed,
and our best work is still to come.
If you've given your best, you're finished!"*

ABU SANDEEP

the golden thread

(Top and above) Wedding outfit, marking the first time Abu Jani Sandeep Khosla used real silver material and real kasab (gold thread). 'Old rose' was an unconventional bridal colour.

When Abu and Sandeep met, they embarked on a journey of discovering the lost crafts and traditions of India in their quest for surface textile developments. This route led them to the doorstep of zardozi. A 'royal' form of embroidery, zardozi comes from Persia and means 'sewing with gold'. While gold embellishments on textiles and furnishings were not new to India, and indeed had been in practice from the time of the *Rig Veda*, it was the Turk-Afghan sultans, and later the Mughals, who brought this exquisitely ornate, glitteringly encrusted, gold threadwork to the India they ruled, soon making it into an imperial craft.

By the 1980s, zardozi had petered out to the quick and easy 'naqshi ka challah' stitch, which made up almost all the heavy, flat embroideries of the day, rendering them unimaginative and repetitively patterned. It was around this time, during his stint with a garments export firm, that Abu first came to meet embroidery artisans. These craftsmen, who still carried the secrets of zardozi, were being wasted by the demands of swift, cheap, high-street embroideries for the Western market, in the form of sheets of sequins making the butterfly tops and dresses with which India was associated. Together, Abu and Sandeep started to take the first steps towards making their dreams and visions a reality – the fantasy of rediscovering the Golden Age of India, when craft was used to create luxurious objects of desire. Zardozi was among the first ancient crafts they encountered on their journey.

When beginning to work on an idea, Abu and Sandeep sit together, by themselves, to conceptualize. Abu then draws the concepts out into embroidery patterns. Next the pair sit with a master embroiderer to set the various zardozi stitches into the pattern. An embroidery swatch is produced to the duo's exacting standards before the final stage of an outfit or a collection is reached. Abu and Sandeep have not only revived many ancient zardozi stitches, they have also modified them and invented new stitches to fill out their intricate embroidery patterns. Their gift for the use of colour has further enhanced their journey into zardozi. It is this single-minded dedication to achieve the best, to rescue and grow ancient Indian crafts to fit into the aesthetics of the modern world, that has struck a chord with clients – the unashamed luxury, beauty and purity.

Abu and Sandeep have made many landmark zardozi wedding garments over the years, and these have been the birth of some of their most famous zardozi lines. One of their first wedding outfits was made in the vasli stitch from the zardozi family in the late 1980s. This beautiful wedding ghagra led them to create a collection dedicated to the stitch. The 'Vasli' line continues to sell out to this day.

The mirror wedding outfit made for Rima Kapoor Jain in 1989 was inspired by the Kutchi mirror work tradition of Gujarat. Abu and Sandeep had mirror specially cut into large, square pieces for an embroidery pattern drawn by Abu. Gold thread replaced the usual multicoloured thread. The 'Mirror Work' line was revisited for the film *Devdas* in the early 2000s, Abu and Sandeep taking their inspiration from the Sheesh Mahal (hall of mirrors) scene in the film *Mughal-e-Azam*, but lifting the concept to another level when the ghagra worn by the courtesan in *Devdas* reflected hundreds of candles in its mirrors. The 'Mirror Work' line continues today, though it has been restructured and redesigned time and again in different avatars. Abu Sandeep's 'Lotus Pond' range has also been presented with mirrors.

The 'Persian Carpet' made especially for Tina Ambani's wedding reception in February 1991 was a one-off creation. Abu and Sandeep drew inspiration from beautiful old Persian carpets, which Abu drew into embroidery patterns. The pair then formed the work with resham thread, chenille embroidery, crystals and stones, all treated to look like a priceless Persian carpet.

(Below) Detail of the 'Dhaka' line of embroidery in pastel shades with resham zardozi embroidery.

(Bottom) Typical zardozi padded detail in various materials, including saadi, naqshi and kora. All these are spring-like metallic materials, which are gold-plated and cut into specific sizes as demanded by the motif.

Abu was in the Middle East, on a trip to meet his aunt, when he chanced upon Swarovski crystals in a shop. Inspired by the lotus pond paintings of renowned contemporary Indian artist A. Ramachandran, Abu and Sandeep used silver crystals and kasab to create the first 'Lotus Pond' outfit for the reception of a young bride in 1993. The outfit was made up of a golden pond of kasab, with floating three-dimensional lotuses encrusted with silver crystals in different sizes. The 'Lotus Pond' collection, which followed long after this first reception outfit, has been presented in many versions, one of the most recent being in gota.

Gota is a woven metallic ribbon that uses gold or silver wire thread and silk or cotton thread. It is made in Gujarat and was formerly used mainly as borders and finishes, and also as flowers and dots on many North Indian royal outfits. Abu and Sandeep gave it their unique twist for the first time on the khadi outfit they made especially for the 'Khadi' exhibition in New Delhi in 2002. It was a traditional Anarkali outfit, with zardozi borders and gota dots all over the fifty metres of khadi of which it was composed. Gota has been a constant in Abu and Sandeep's work over the years, and they have kept reinventing its usage on fabric with much success.

Zardozi with resham and gold threads mixed together on French silk tulle formed another exquisite line of saris created by the pair in the early 1990s. This classic line has also been revisited in the recent past in versions of gota.

In addition, Abu and Sandeep have produced the 'Stone' ranges on silk tulle. Stones of various shapes, sizes and colours are patterned all over blouses to create the illusion of the stones being attached to the skin. The designers' love for stones has showed up in a lot of their work. They have used precious materials, such as rubies, emeralds and freshwater pearls, in some very specialized outfits for some highly exclusive clients. It is this same passion for stones that led to the 'Jewelled' collection in their early years. They covered up the body with long, embroidered sleeves and bodices like a second skin, while choker-like collars took the place of real jewelry. In fact, a collection with Swarovski crystal collars was aimed to replace the diamond necklace! The 'Raaga' line, meanwhile, was made especially for women to show off their earrings, since a heavily embroidered gold or silver yoke took the place of necklaces and heavily embroidered cuffs took the place of bracelets. The concept went down well and the outfits flew off the racks. The 'Deco' line, inspired by a ruby and diamond brooch bought by Abu, featured sari drapes with sheets of stones making up Art Deco patterns, with another highly distinctive Art Deco pattern running as a border.

Aari is another ancient form of embellishment used by Abu and Sandeep. Before they came along, this straight running stitch, made with a hook-shaped needle, was regarded as a relatively simple form of embroidery. As with chikan and zardozi, Abu and Sandeep improvised and invented new ways to use the stitch. They mixed it with zardozi to create one of their longest running ranges, inspired by an old silk-thread embroidery from the state of Bengal, dating back to the early colonial period and made for a European. When Abu and Sandeep conceived this intricate floral range, they named it 'Dhaka' (now the capital of Bangladesh).

The 'Bharatpore' line was first conceived in 1988, when a bride came to Abu and Sandeep for a wedding outfit and confessed her love of birds to them. They created a ghagra featuring dense foliage and beautiful birds, embroidered in resham zardozi and embellished with crystals, stones and sequins. When Abu and Sandeep made the first collection of this range, in an aari zardozi mix, they named it 'Bharatpore', after the world-famous Bharatpur bird sanctuary in Rajasthan. Their 'Kehkashan', 'Agra', 'Jamevar' and 'Carpet' ranges were also a mix of aari and zardozi. Pure aari lines include the 'Balinesian', or 'Dancing Dolls', collection (a trip to Bali, with its striking architecture, art and old textiles, inspired Abu to draw the famous dancing dolls).

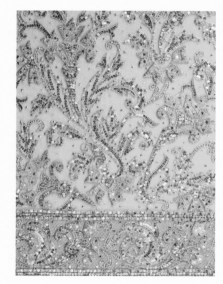

Other lines made using aari include the suzani-inspired 'Bedouin' collection, as well as the 'Kilm' and 'Fiza' collections.

Around 1993–94, Abu and Sandeep accompanied some clients, who had become friends, on a trip to Tharad. The friends were part of the diamond community, which was very involved in this part of Gujarat, around forty kilometres from Pakistan. As Tharad is often hit by drought, the community were trying to set up various money-making schemes for the local people, who up until then had been dependent on agriculture. Droughts made earning a livelihood very difficult. Abu and Sandeep wanted to see if they could help in any way. They were aware of the colourful rural Gujarati embroideries and soon became convinced that they could set something up in the locality. They handed over fabrics such as crêpe de chine and chiffon to some of the local women and asked them to use their regular stitches, but also gave them directions on the formation of the motifs and borders and in addition on the colours. Over the years, with direction and a lot of patience, production of the 'Tharad' line has continued, but the work has become much finer. New embroidery patterns have been drawn out by Abu especially for the ladies, and new stitches have been introduced. Most importantly the line has helped battle the grim consequences of drought.

For Abu and Sandeep, the finish of their garments is just as important as the surface embroidery. For one of their photo shoots (see p. 89), the garment was worn inside out and it is impossible to tell the difference. A typical Abu Sandeep wedding ghagra is made three to four inches short in order to leave space for finishes and borders to be added. In fact, the duo have developed a whole range of saris with multiple zardozi borders. Even their 'Pink City' range, inspired by Jaipur, has beautiful leheriya stripes as the finish of the garments.

Abu and Sandeep's meticulous and thoughtful attention to detail also extends to creating a harmonious and secure atmosphere for all the craftsmen that work with them. Even though the majority are from the central and eastern states of India, Eid-Ul-Fitr and Diwali are celebrated every year and all the factory workers, along with their families, participate in the celebrations.

Abu and Sandeep continue to expand the crafts they use every day, just as they continue to pick up crafts that have been waylaid by the demand for 'quick'. They often give their lines and collections the name of the stitch they have been nurturing, or they name the line or collection after the area from which the individual craft comes. More often, however, it is the pair's adventurous and lyrical nature that takes over the 'naming' ceremonies, which also include the presence of the Abu Jani Sandeep Khosla team. This forms a way for the team to get to know one another and to establish a personal connection. Abu and Sandeep particularly enjoy evoking a feeling of the old world, the unexplored, the opulent luxuries of days gone by, a depth of thought … and they like to offer salutations to the people and places that have inspired them. Once, when a sample of colourful embroidery patterns was finished, they were reminded of the beautiful patola saris of Gujarat (it is said that the finest take over a year to be hand-woven), and so they named their collection 'Patola'. The 'Isfahan' collection, on the other hand, had nothing to do with the famous blue pottery found in the area; it was so called because when Abu and Sandeep looked at the rich profusion of flowers on the sample, they were reminded of Persia, and the name Isfahan was rich with the 'feeling' of Persia.

And so continue the diverse and intricate embroidered collections, with their equally diverse names, from the Abu Jani Sandeep Khosla label. Abu and Sandeep's love affair with Indian luxury is eternal, as is their commitment to keeping remarkable crafts and traditions alive.

(Top) Bridal outfit, featuring zardozi and metallic gold thread (see also pp. 344–45).

(Above) Sequins outlined with silver dori (twisted thread) and lace embroidery.

(Opposite) Gold jewelled dress, hand-embroidered with pieces of metal inspired by South Indian gold jewelry.

Panelled skirt in turquoise-green crêpe de chine, with an embroidery of glass beads and sequins, and silk thread on ruched gold lace forming the embroidery pattern.

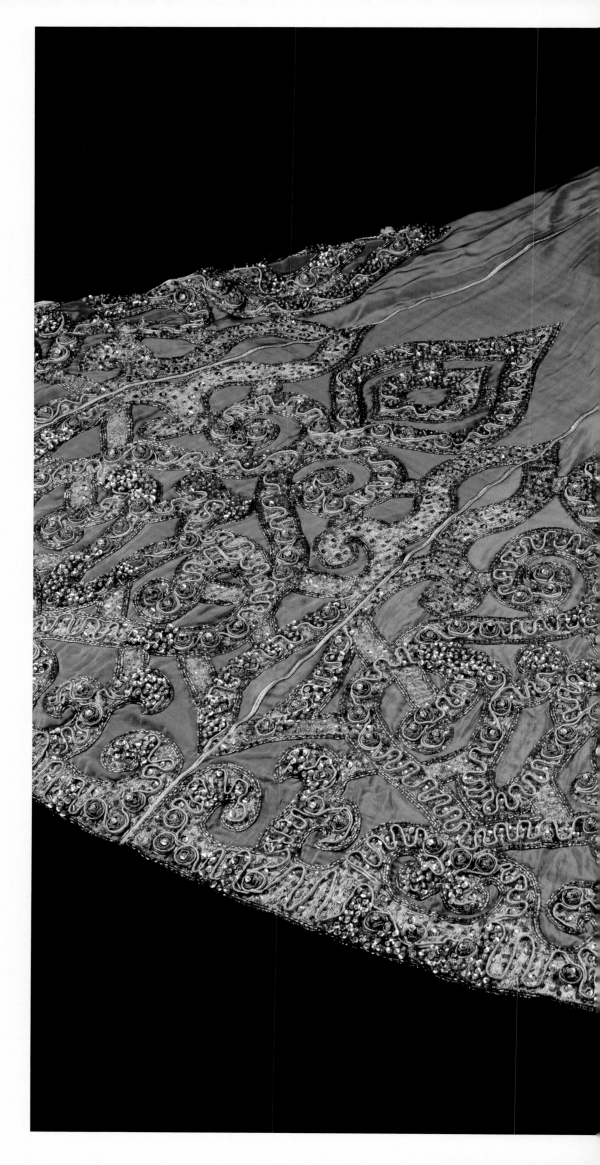

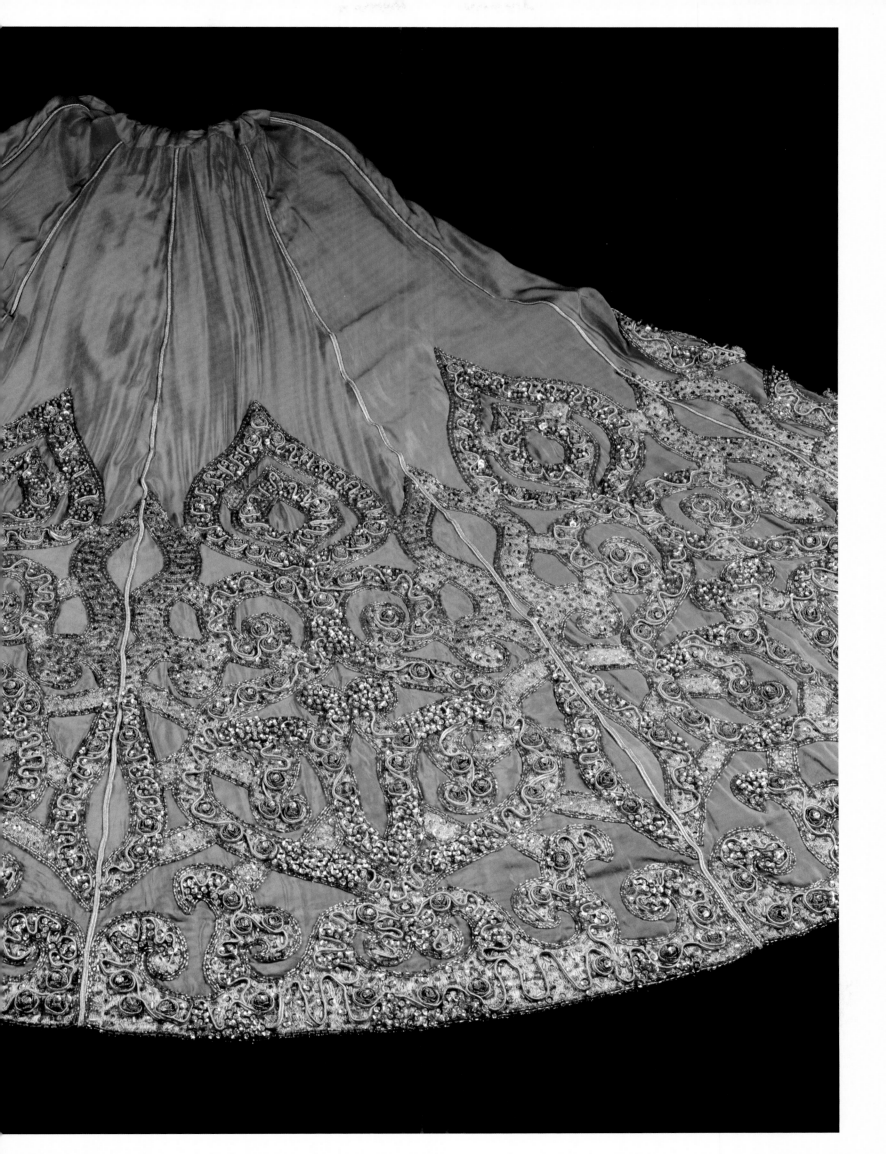

Vasli lehenga made with touches of metallic materials treated entirely in zardozi to form a graded leaf pattern like that found on the inside of domes.

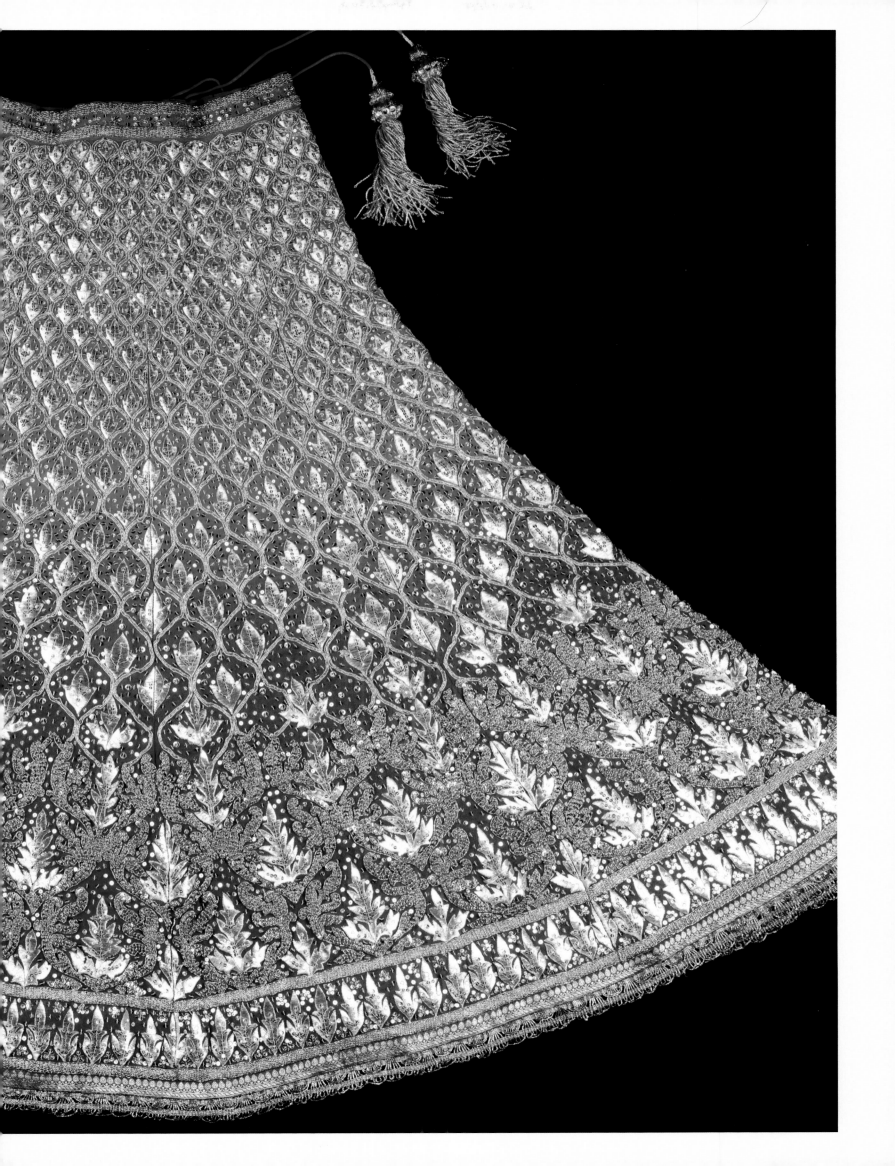

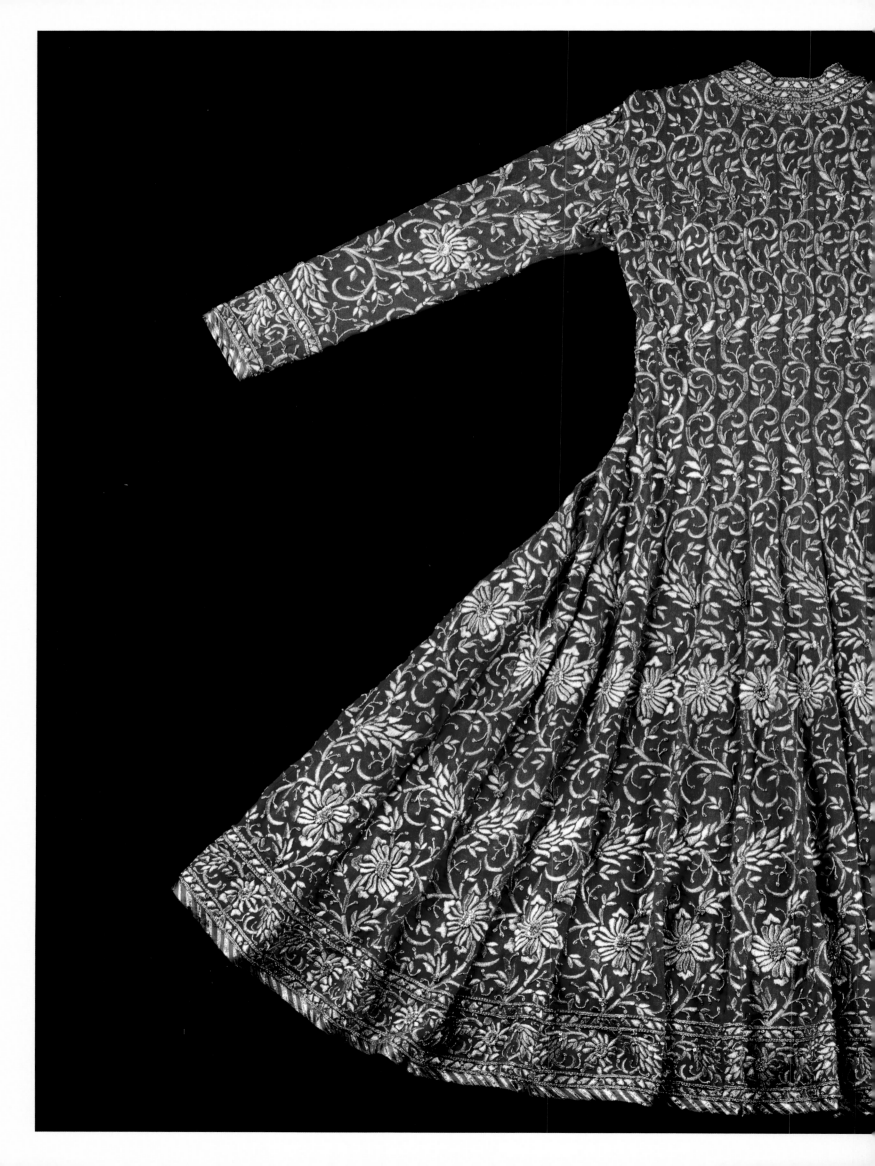

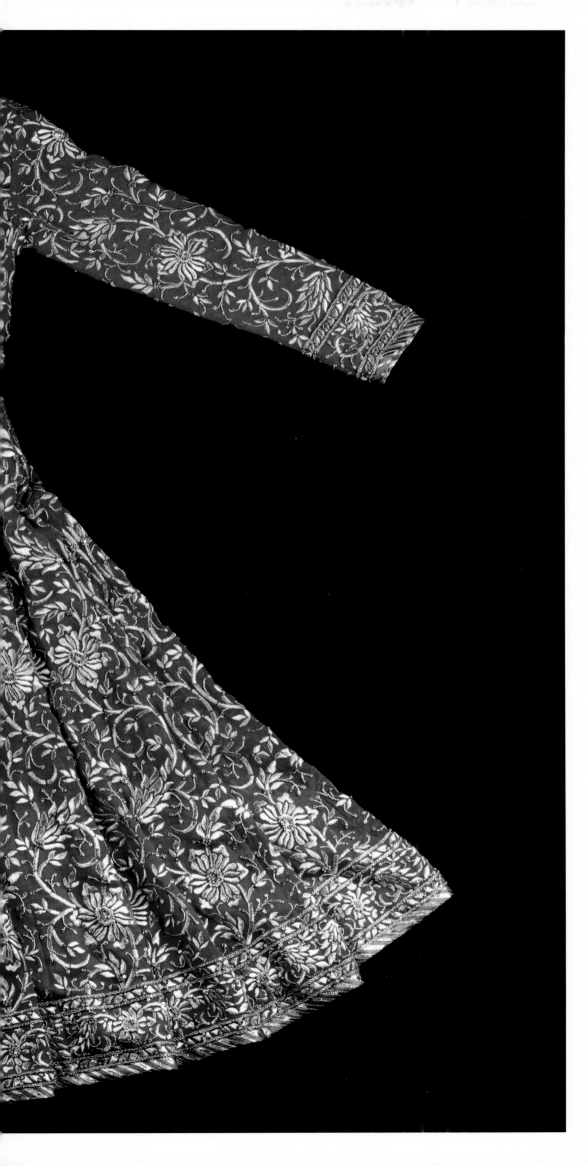

Multipanelled silk coat with a thick border at the cuffs and hem, a graded embroidery pattern all over and an embroidered bordered detail around the neck.

Swarovski-encrusted wedding lehenga from the '3D Stone' line, featuring three-dimensional motifs of fantasy lotus flowers.

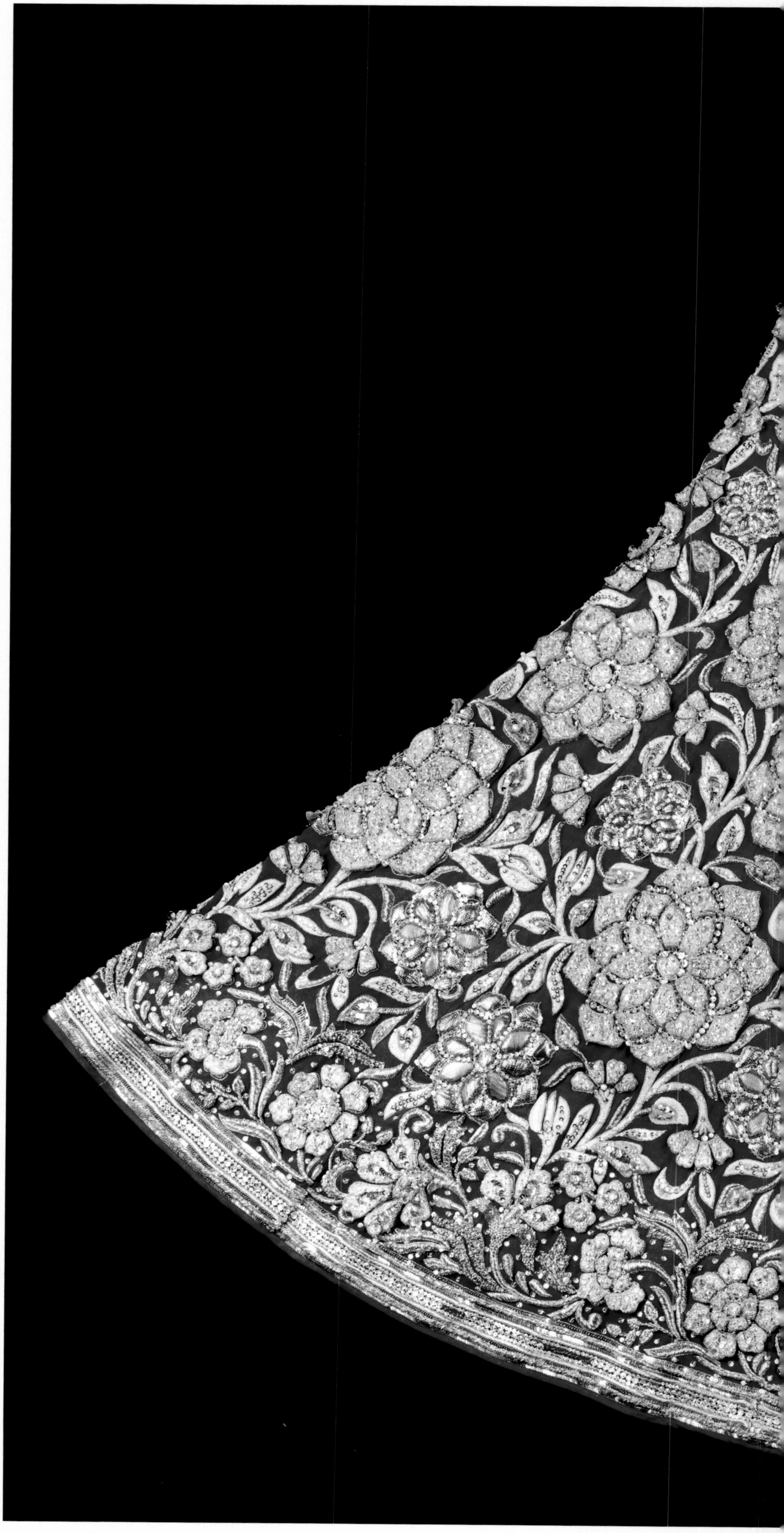

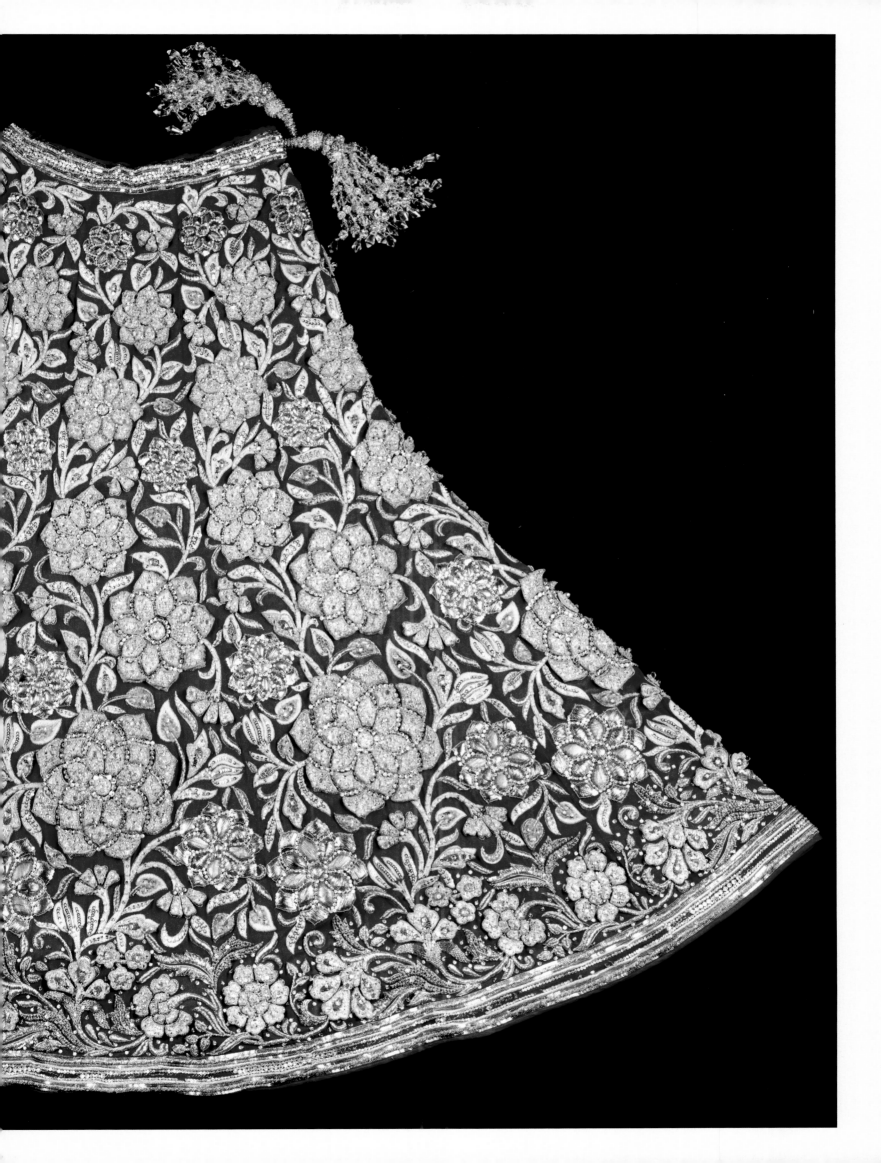

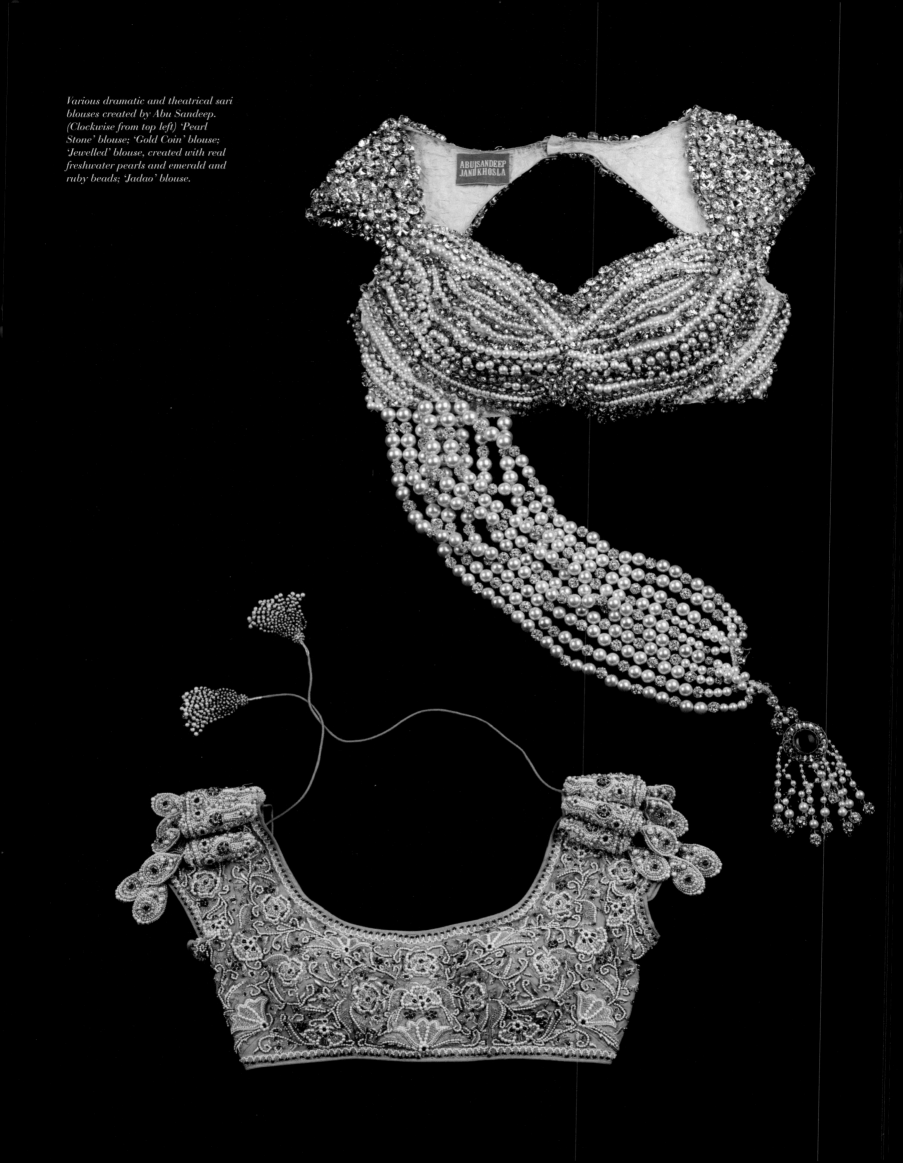

Various dramatic and theatrical sari blouses created by Abu Sandeep. (Clockwise from top left) 'Pearl Stone' blouse; 'Gold Coin' blouse; 'Jewelled' blouse, created with real freshwater pearls and emerald and ruby beads; 'Jadao' blouse.

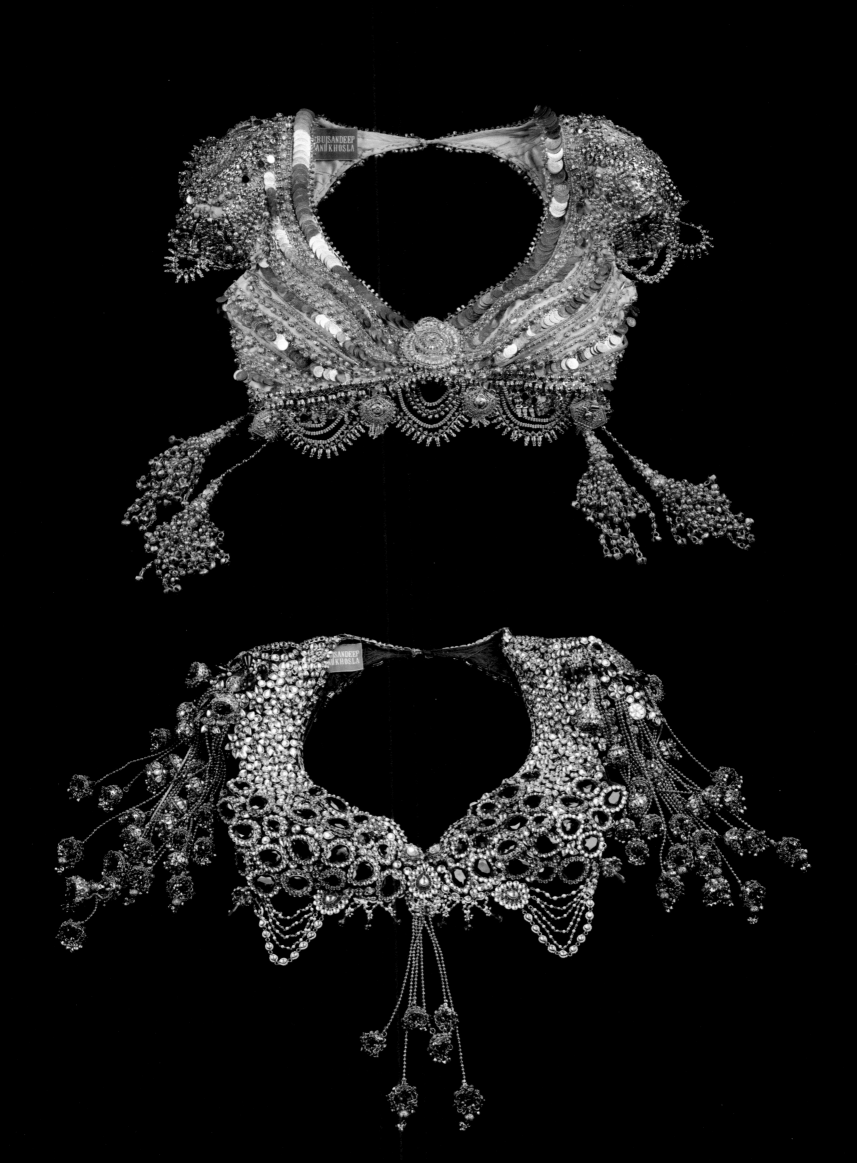

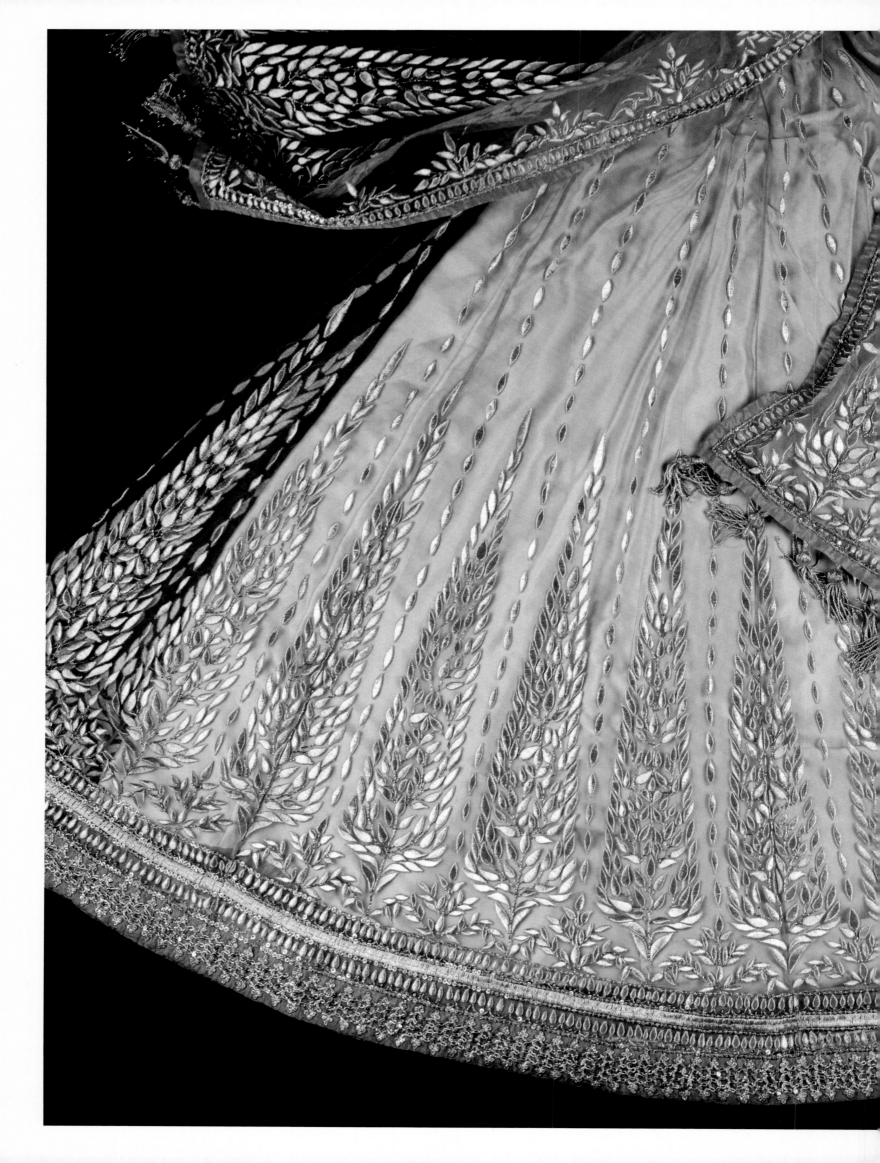

Vasli ghagra made on silk tulle, with a dupatta featuring edges trimmed with zardozi metalwork tassels. The pattern was Abu's version of the 'Tree of Life'.

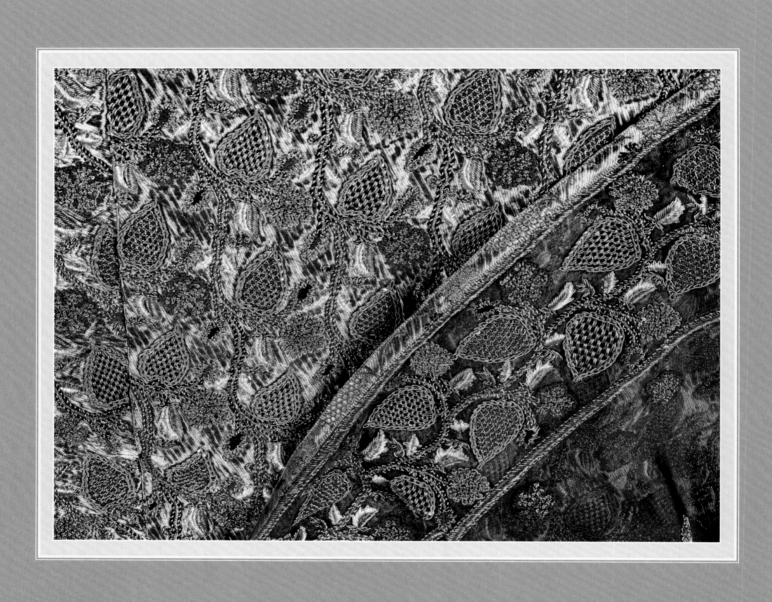

Detail of zardozi work in metal thread done on rich khinkhaab brocade.
The dupatta edge is trimmed with churi stitches in zardozi.

Wedding lehenga in lace, with zardozi and silk thread embroidery
following a similar pattern on the lace itself.

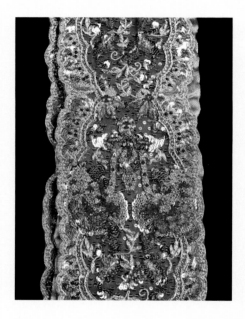

Asymmetrical double-layered sequin and zardozi lehenga with red crystal stones.

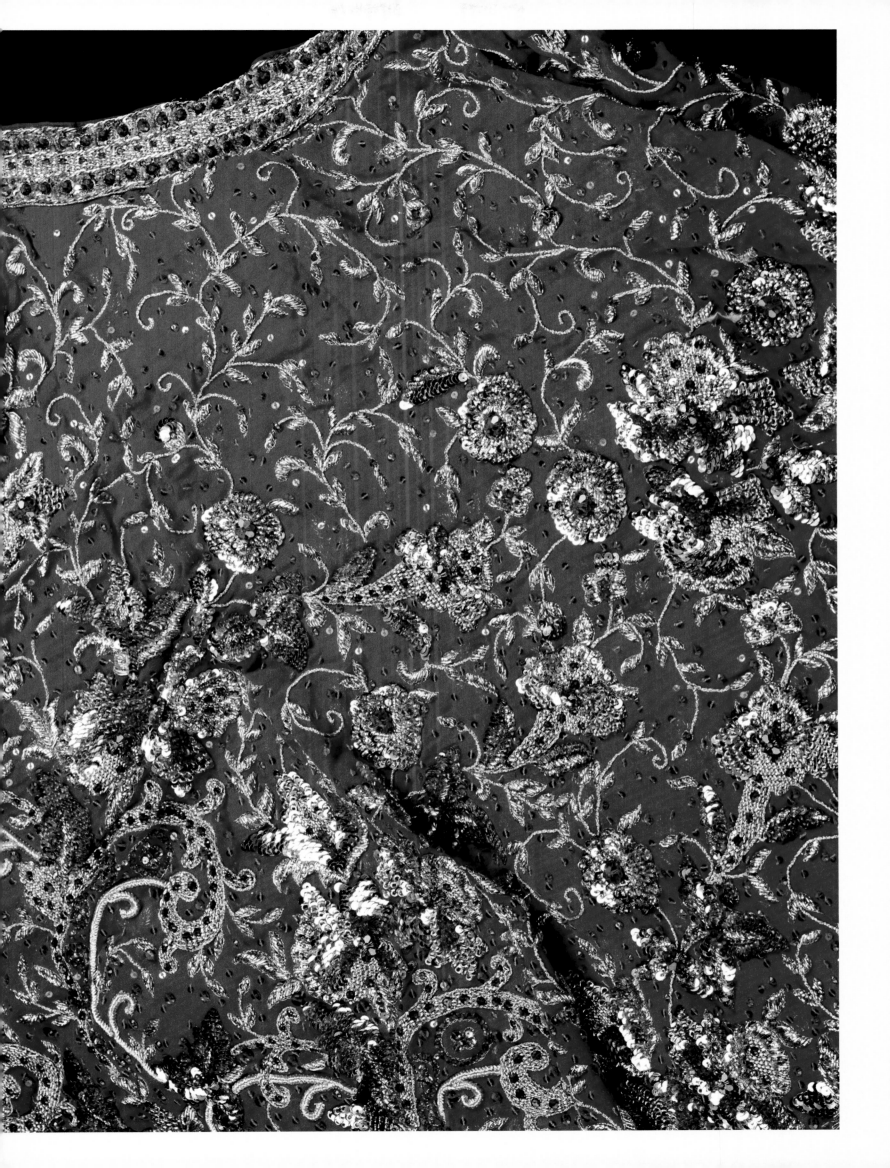

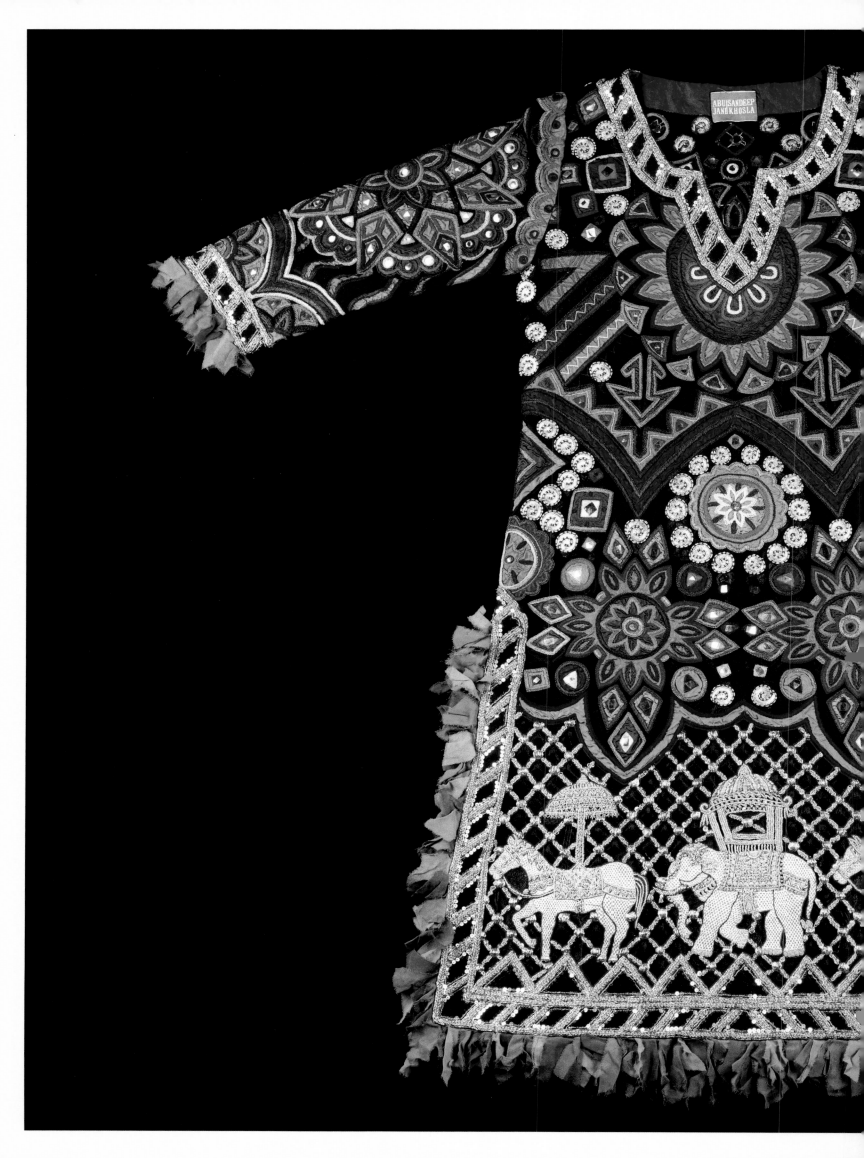

Multicoloured earth-toned appliquéd 'Exotica' tunic, with a zardozi procession of horses and elephants at the base. The garment has been finished with chindis (scraps).

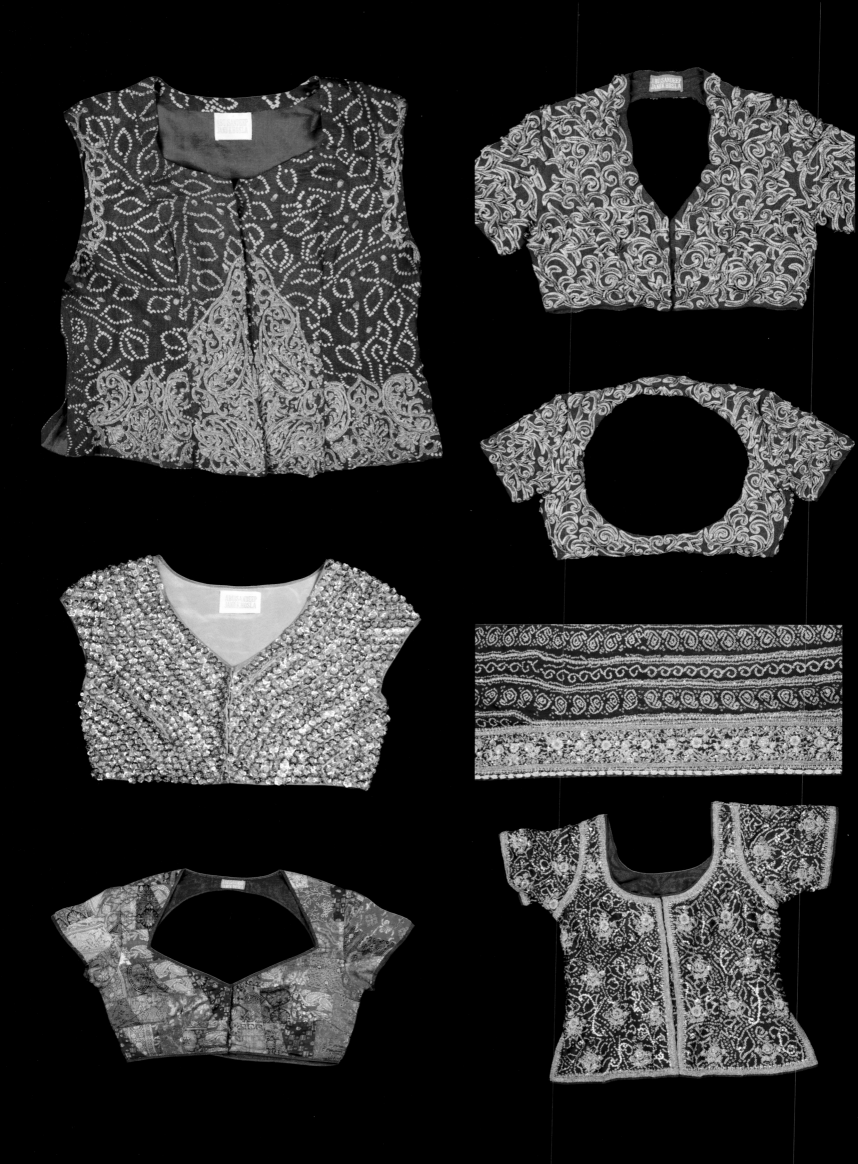

Various blouses created by Abu Sandeep. (Opposite, clockwise from top left) Blouse with marodi work on bandhini fabric; front and back of a blouse with jaal done in padded badla work; dupatta and blouse with intricate zardozi work and churi borders at the edges; brocade patchwork blouse; gota detail blouse. (This page, clockwise from left) Blouse with three-dimensional gota embroidery; boat-necked sleeveless blouse embroidered with dangling pearls and glass beads; back and front of a blouse from the 'Rabadi' line, embroidered with thread and gold matt and metallic threads to form a pattern inspired by the nomadic tribes of Gujarat; blouse with tailoring details and hand-appliquéd gota.

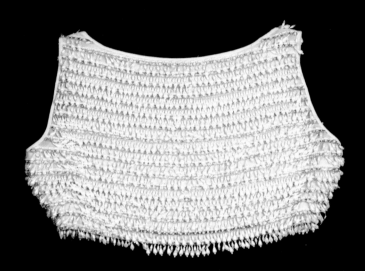

Various swatches of specially designed border finishes, an Abu Sandeep speciality. (This page, above and below) Zardozi chotla (plait), crochet and sequins; gota with silk. (Opposite, clockwise from top left) Gota appliquéd on silk; types of gota and silk detail; silk appliqués; Jaipuri gota patti tailoring detail.

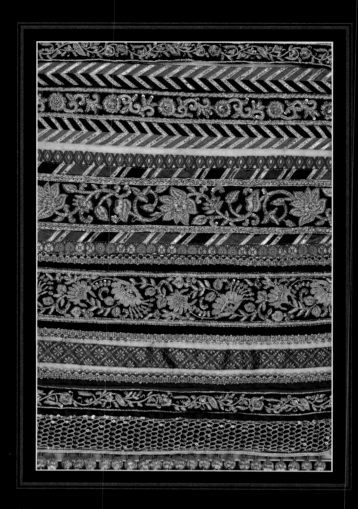

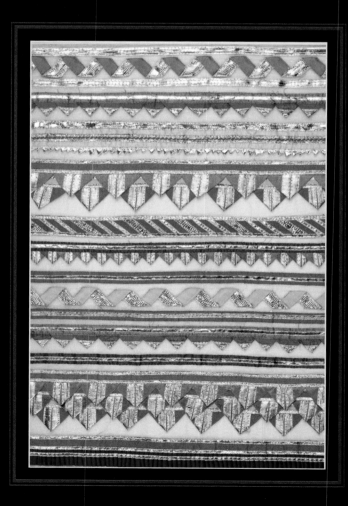

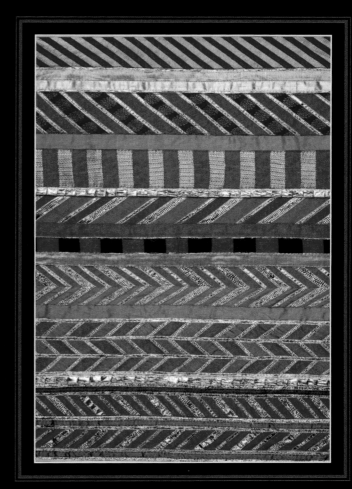

(Opposite) Wedding lehenga of a fine silk bandhini fabric, with intricate zardozi embroidery and a churi border at the base.

(Below) Typical Marwari bridegroom's accessories: cummerbund, jooties (shoes), gathjoda (to bind the groom and bride together) and angvastra (shawl), all made with pure silver and freshwater pearls.

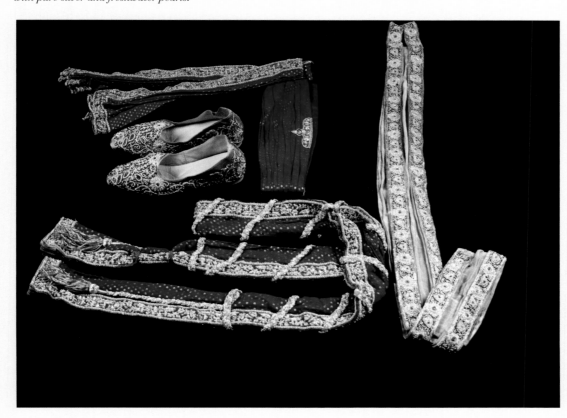

*Sample panel of roses peeping out of an intricate and tight mesh of flowers and leaves,
shaded in gold, with silk threads on deep coloured silk velvet.*

Sample panel, drawing inspiration from European lace and a baroque style,
embroidered in silk thread with gold metal material.

Bandhgala jacket of fine wool, with silk thread aari and zardozi embroidery.

Sherwani with yoke, in real silver and freshwater pearls.

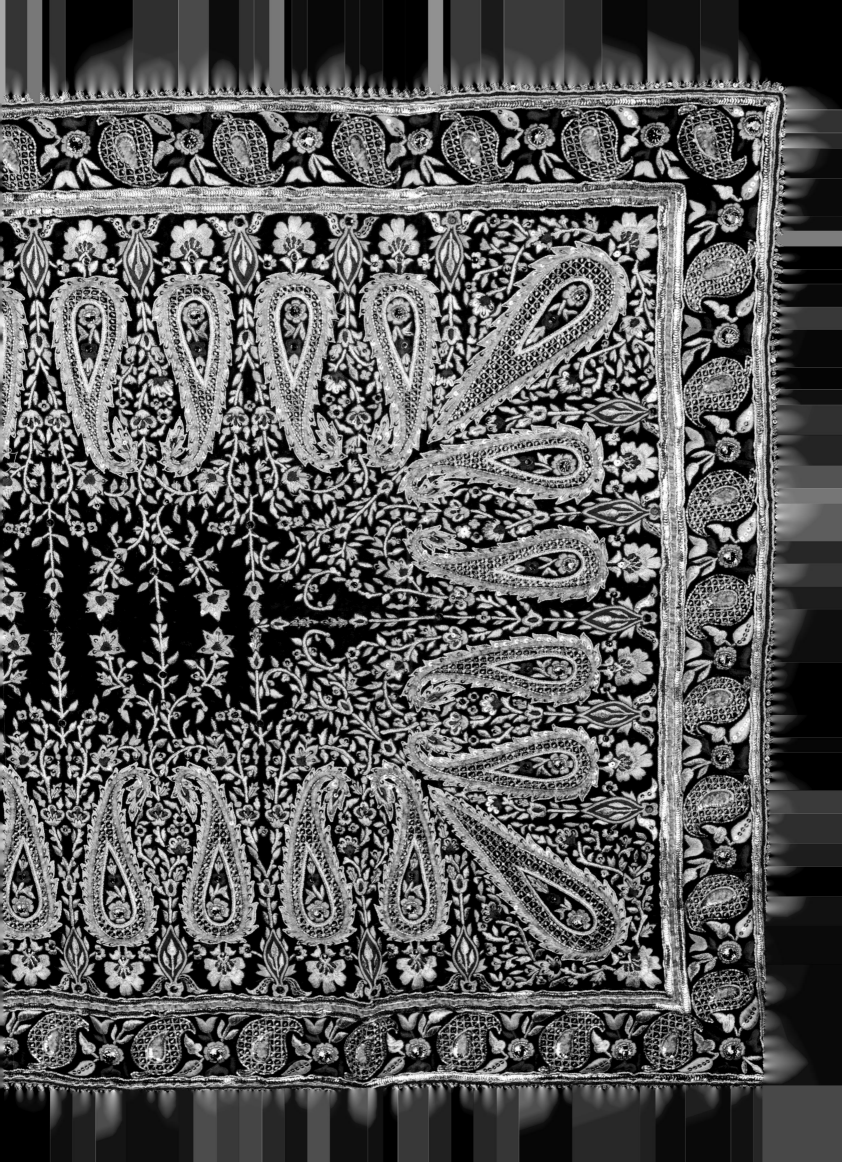

(Previous pages) Large wedding shawl inspired by the Jamevar paisley, worked here in gold materials (kasab, saadi, naqshi and kora), French knots and padded silk thread.

(Below left) Sample of pure zardozi embroidery.

(Below right) Sample of pure vasli embroidery, the border featuring a mix of vasli and zardozi embroidery.

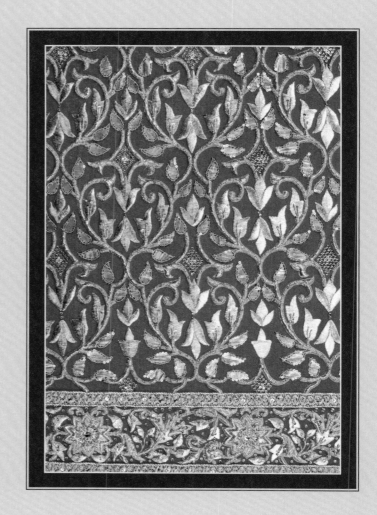

(Below left) Sample of zardozi with pearl embroidery.

(Below right) Sample of twisted gold thread done in marodi embroidery, with the border in gold dori (cord).

Sample featuring almost all the stitches of zardozi, padded and also flat.

Sample showing a typical example of doke (kasab padding) with zardozi.

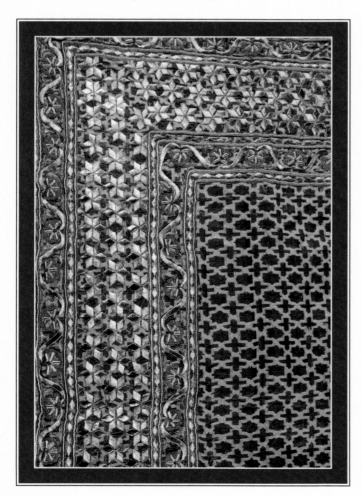

Vasli stars done in kasab doke on the border of a Benarasi jamdani fabric.

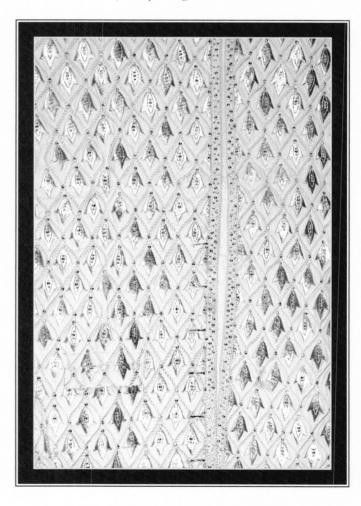

Sample of vasli with metal sequins on a boski fabric.

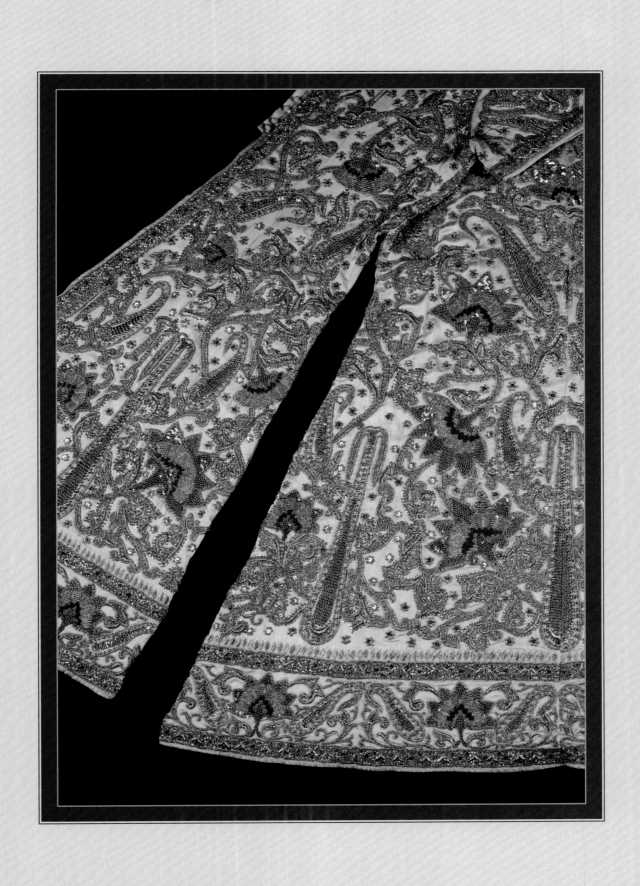

Section of a dramatic coat styled in the Oriental manner
with one of Abu Sandeep's typical embroideries in zardozi.

Examples of Abu Sandeep's inspirations from traditional drawings put into embroidery.

(Page 316) Zardozi sample on a bandhini fabric during the embroidery process; the outlines for the embroidery work can be seen.

(Page 317) Rich, pure zardozi sample with touches of Swarovski crystals on a heavy silk velvet fabric.

(Opposite) Section of a fuchsia pink sari done in zardozi and resham, from the 'Heavenly Haathi' range.

(Following pages) Detail of a wedding outfit, marking the first time Abu and Sandeep introduced a men's bandhgala sherwani (high closed-collar coat) for a bride. Consisting of ten metres of maroon pure silk georgette velvet, with Abu and Sandeep's version of a Persian carpet embroidered on it in earth colours, the garment is ankle-length with an extra flare, and was worn with a flared tunic in brocade underneath.

Tunic from the 'Bharatpore' line, done in pure silk thread zardozi embroidery.

Pure resham zardozi embroidery in multicolours from the 'Dhaka' range.

Various examples of silk thread embroidery in zardozi and aari on silk georgette fabrics. (This page, above and below) From the 'Sarah' line; from the 'Naqah' line. (Opposite, clockwise from top left) From the 'Inlay' line; from the 'Jamevar' line; from the 'Coloured Resham' line; from the 'Sarah' line.

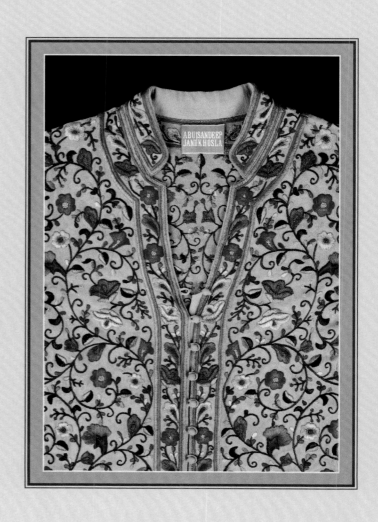

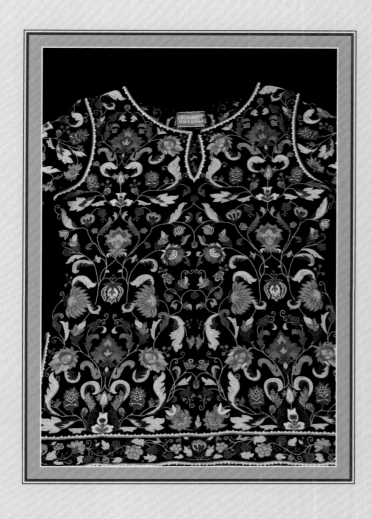

Detail of the 'Africa' line, silk thread embroidery done in pure aari.

Detail of the 'Africa' line, silk thread embroidery done in pure aari.

Four details of the 'Tharad' line, with mirror work and silk thread in chain stitch.

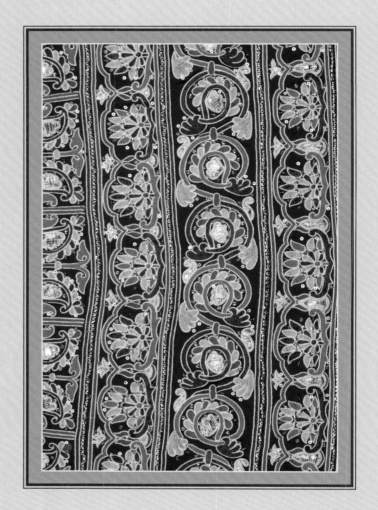

Details of Abu and Sandeep's early works in resham embroidery. (Below, left to right) Detail on silk georgette from the 'Jamevar' range; detail of a scarf in chamois satin from the 'Dori' line, essentially embroidery with a twisted silk cord; detail of a yoke on a blouse on woollen fabric from the 'Dori' line.

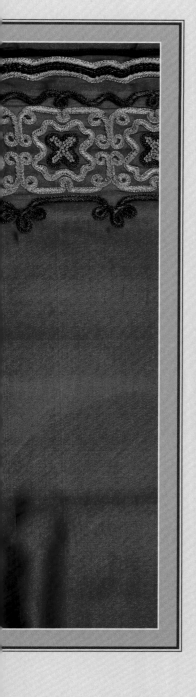

Detail of embroidery in pure resham aari chain stitch for the 'Kitsch' line, inspired by abstract drawings made by Abu and Sandeep for their 'Africa' Art Wear collection.

Detail of the 'Faces' line, based on a fashion sketch,
which evolved into a mosaic embroidery in resham thread in aari.

Resham embroidery in zardozi on silk georgette.

Resham embroidery with a sprinkling of sequins and crystals in zardozi on silk georgette.

Chrysanthemum flowers done in twisted silk thread in zardozi on khinkhaab brocade.

Detail of the 'Bharatpore' line done in resham thread in aari.

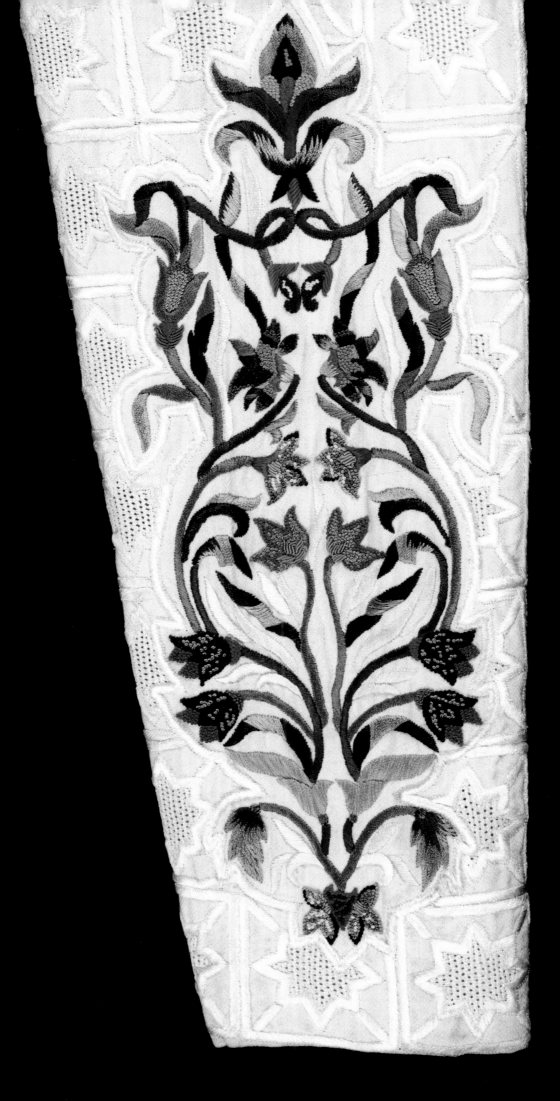

*Detail of a sleeve with cotton thread zardozi embroidery on cotton fabric,
inspired by the pietra dura in the Taj Mahal.*

Detail of an outfit from the 'Jamevar' line, embroidery in cotton resham thread on woollen fabric.

Detail of an outfit from the 'Jamevar' line, embroidery in cotton resham thread on woollen fabric.

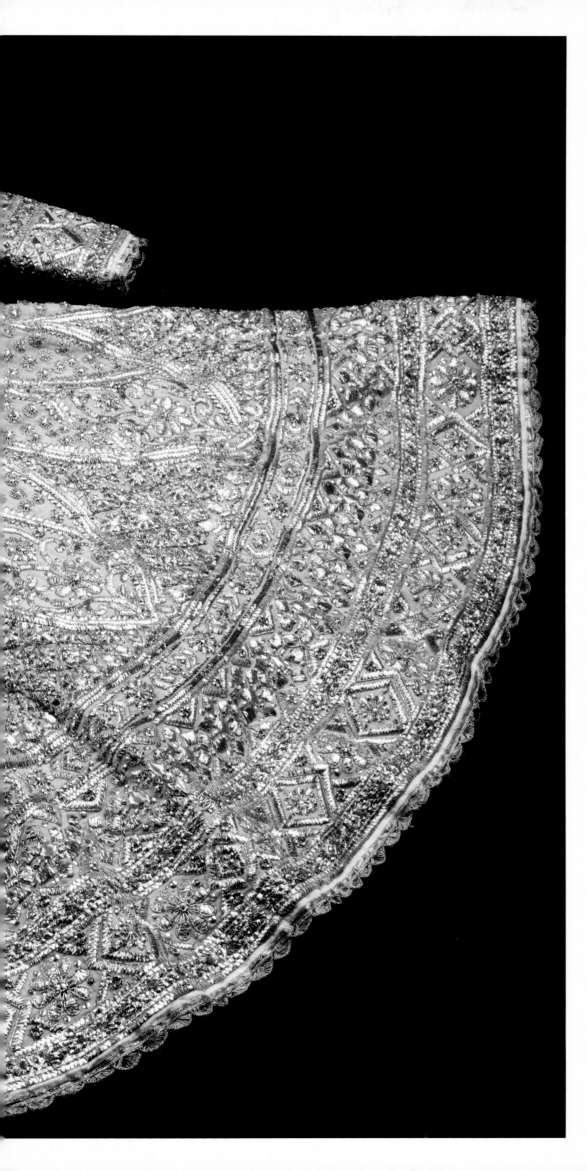

Limited edition outfit from the 'All-Out Gota' collection, specially embroidered on very fine khadi fabric.

Detail of a sari palloo from the 'Mahi Gota' line, made up of multiple borders and appliqués of silk georgette with gota work applied.

Detail of the 'Gota Tukdi' line done in pure zardozi embroidery.
Here, the gota is glued onto paper, then cut according to the drawing and appliquéd onto the fabric.

Detail of the 'New Gota' range, with stems and small leaves done in badla.
Here, the gota is starched, then cut according to the embroidery pattern and appliquéd onto the fabric.

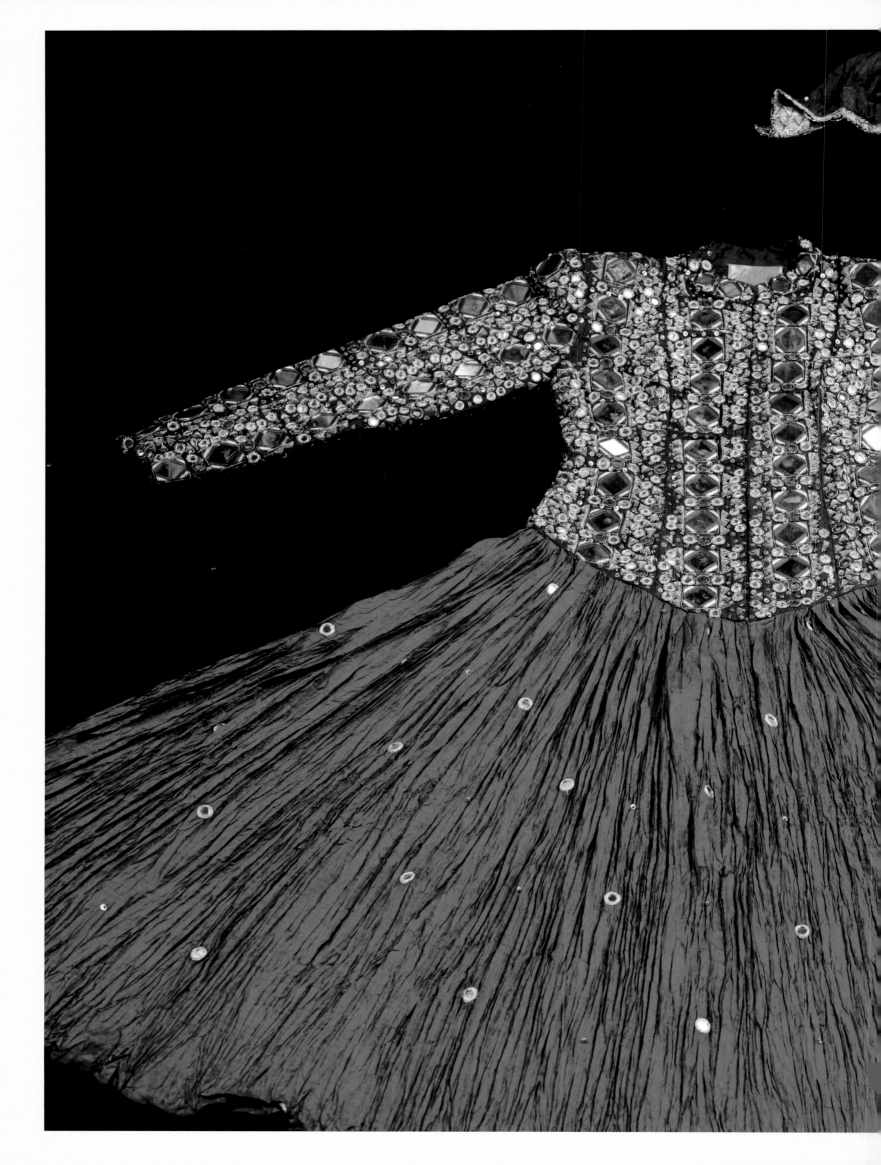

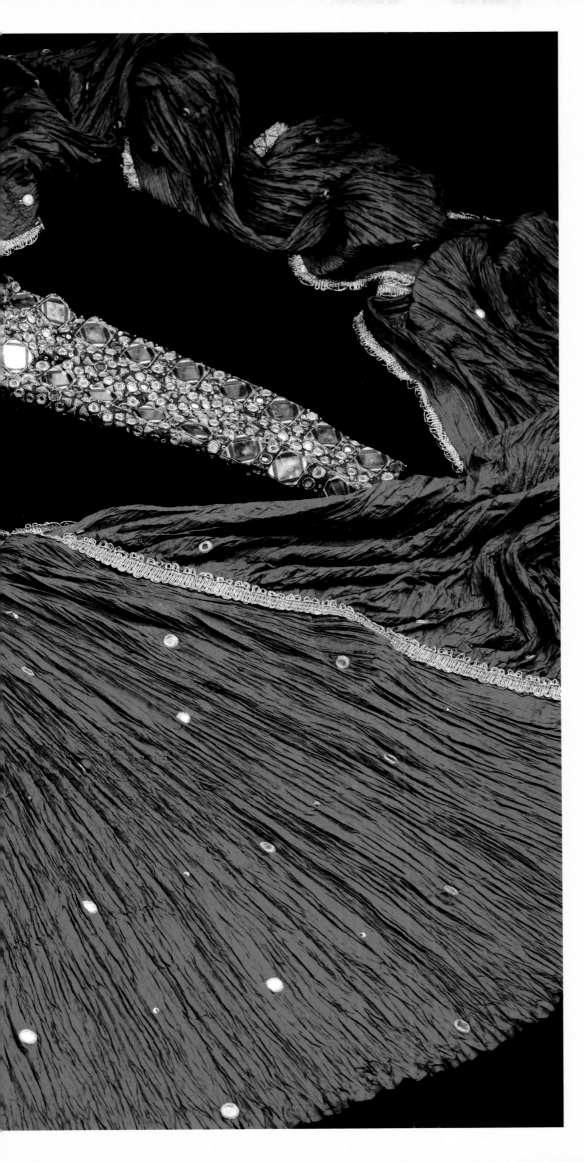

Bridal outfit in crushed silk, marking the first time Abu and Sandeep used mirror work, inspired by the Kutchi work from Gujarat. The body is embellished with square mirrors, surrounded by assorted gold materials, with mirrors sparsely dotted on the crushed flare.

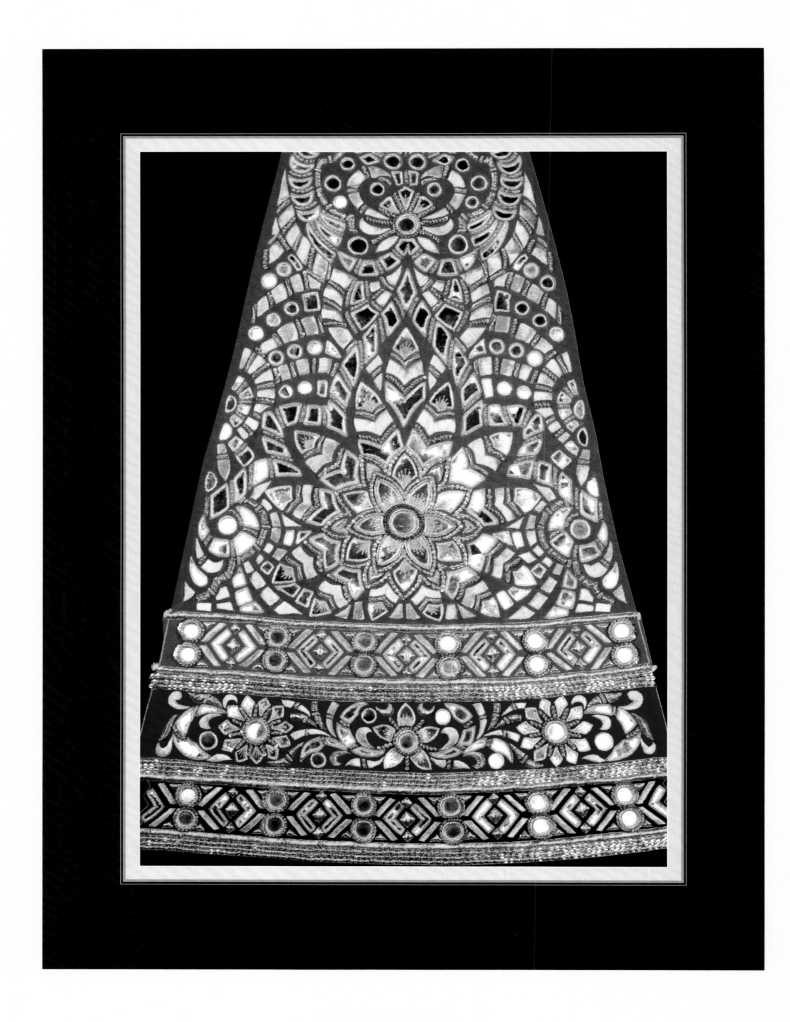

(Above and opposite) Details of a 'Mirror Work' kali (panel) sample.

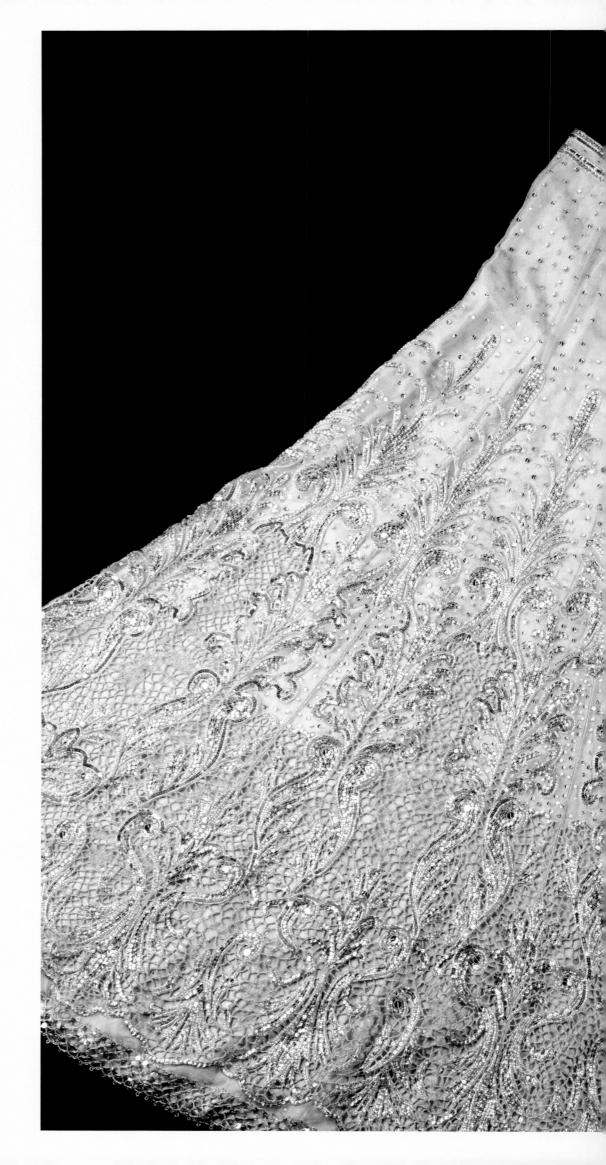

A wedding lehenga that was Abu and Sandeep's first 'Lotus Pond' creation, and a fusion of Orient and Occident. The base, around ten metres of Benares silk organza, was worked entirely in gold and silver thread in kasab and aari, and the lotus blooms were crafted from Swarovski crystals.

Detail of a bridal 'Lotus Pond' outfit made of gold kasab and Swarovski crystal, every inch of the outfit covered in embroidery.

Detail of a lotus from the 'Lotus Pond' bridal outfit (larger detail shown opposite).

Aari zardozi embroidery: an example of Abu and Sandeep inventing a new form of aari.

Western-inspired designs done with various materials, including silk thread, sequins and beads. The final detail shows flowers and buds with an appliqué of three-dimensional organza.

(Below left) Detail of the 'Scroll' line, done in aari with sequins of two different shapes: the stitching goes in one straight vertical line and the sequins change according to the embroidery patterns.

(Below right) Example of a sari with the body worked in diamond-shaped bootis in sequins and the border borrowed from the 'Deco' line.

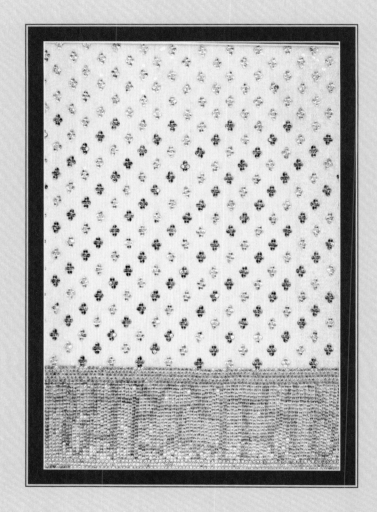

Detail of a sari palloo from the 'Deco' line. The border is done entirely in Swarovski crystals in zardozi embroidery and the body is a sheet of sequins of two kinds, raised and flat, in aari embroidery on silk georgette.

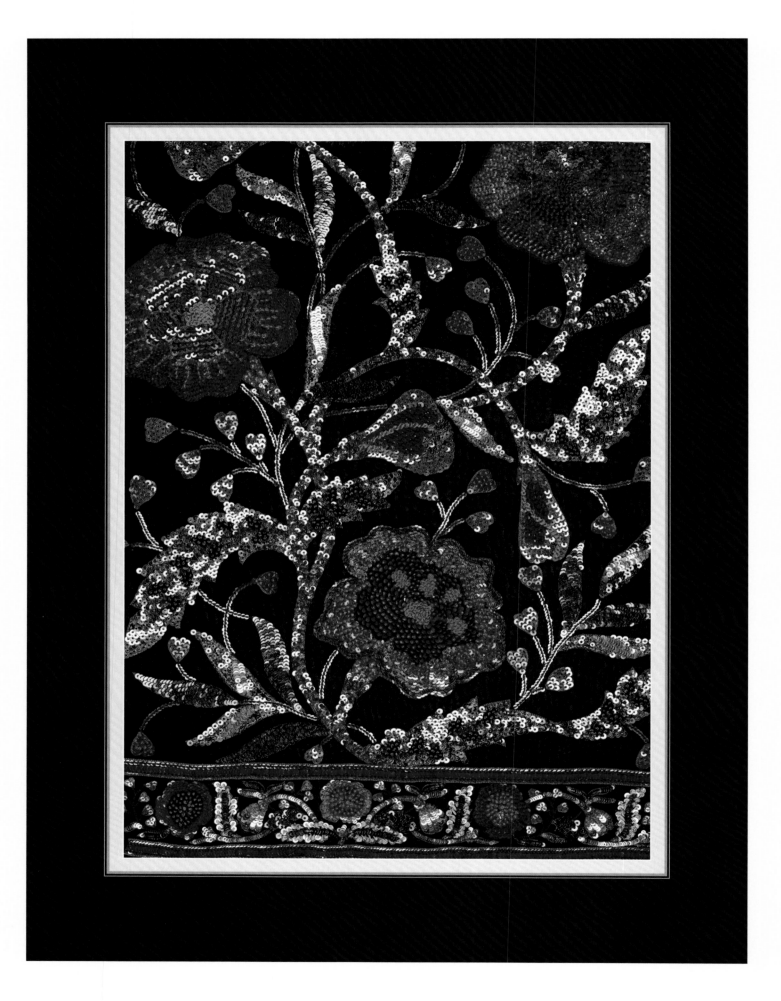

*Example of the 'Shabb' range, in a mix of aari and zardozi stitches
with flat and overlapped sequins and French knots in silk.*

Example of the 'Shabb' range, in a mix of aari and zardozi stitches with flat and overlapped sequins and French knots in silk.

(Below left) Peacocks embroidered against a mesh of peacock feathers, all done in sequins on a lemon georgette fabric.

(Below right) Floral jaal done in stones with aari embroidery.

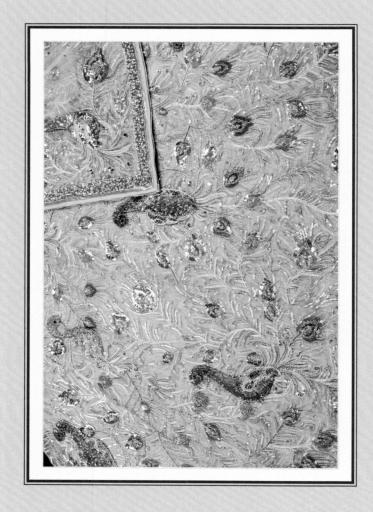

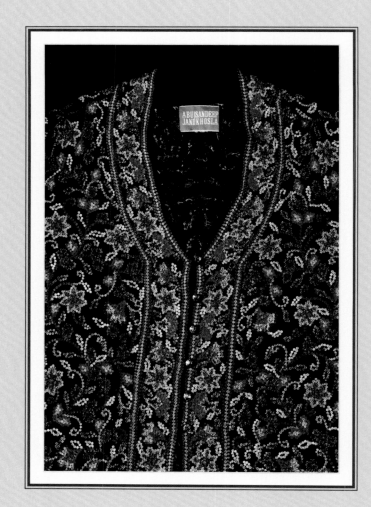

A skirt featuring sequins, resham, cutdaana (a smaller version of bugle beads), glass beads and Swarovski crystals, worked in a mix of aari and zardozi embroidery.

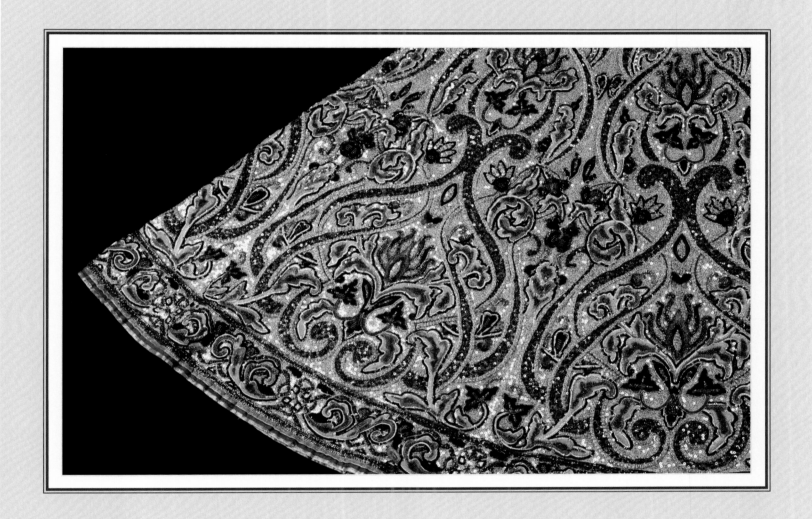

Various examples of borders and finishes developed exclusively by Abu Sandeep.

(Below left) Samples of zardozi borders that are used to finish dupattas and saris.

(Below right) Samples of pearl and sequin borders with silk appliqués to use as finishes on various garments.

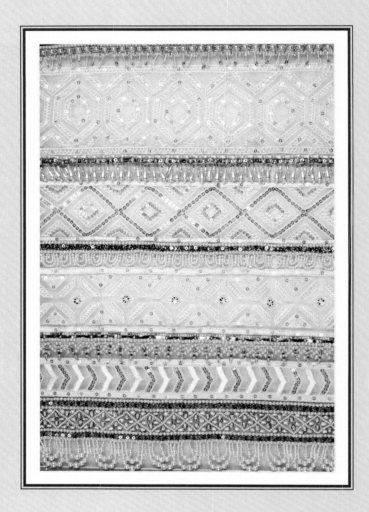

(Below left) Samples of borders done in sequins, silk threads and gota.

(Below right) Samples of appliqués of silk and gota done in tailoring details on organza silk as borders.

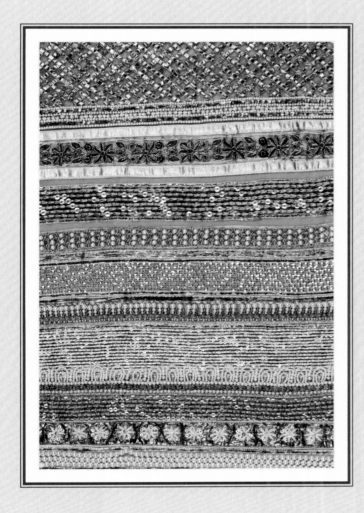

tribute

Simply put: 'the Boys' are the best. There is an eloquence in all that they create, which is rare and unique. I use the word 'eloquence' and not 'elegance'. Several designers in India create elegant garments. But only Abu Sandeep manage to make their garments speak! Mind you, it really is the garments that do the talking … the wearer is merely the vehicle. When you are an Abu Sandeep loyalist, you don't have to say a thing. You merely float into the room for conversation to stop and the clothes to take over the rest of the communication. That's how it has always been for this talented duo.

I can't call myself an Abu Sandeep loyalist, alas, but I do possess two outstanding examples of their work that bear ample testimony to their refined design sensibilities. Where does such inspiration come from? Can quiet understated good taste be taught at a reputed international school of fashion? Does anyone really acquire such deep and abiding knowledge of craft skills going back centuries working in a Parisian atelier with a genius designer? Can a similar passion for all that is beautiful in the world be passed on by someone else? Impossible! Abu Sandeep's aesthetic is distinctly their own. And one only has to recognize their immense talent for what it really is — a divine gift. 'The Boys' are blessed. Their art remains as ethereal and undiminished as it was when they began their fascinating voyage into the unknown, eccentric, egotistical world of fashion twenty-five years ago. How fortunate they are! And it is because of this precious gift that their label has seen the sort of appreciation only a few designers experience during their lifetime. The only reason the two have been able to maintain their supremacy in the brittle and highly competitive world of couture is because of their unshakeable self-belief and commitment to their art. It is indeed a sign of true confidence when senior designers such as Abu Sandeep refuse to go along with whatever is au courant or trendy, preferring to stick to their métier, and still succeed in holding their own, leaving panic attacks to lesser beings.

Their work is their meditation. It shows in the meticulous attention to detail that remains a hallmark of their label. Perfectionism always pays. Experts may spend hours deconstructing the Abu Sandeep magic and analyzing their various 'periods' according to the cuts and craft skills they showcased along the way. But the truth of the matter is more basic. Abu Sandeep are timeless. I possess precisely two saris designed by them, and I love both. I love them enough to be really, really possessive about them … which means I deny access to my own daughters, who otherwise have a free run of my wardrobe. I own some other equally wonderful saris, but the Abu Sandeeps remain special. One day, I shall pass them on to Anasuya Devi, my granddaughter. Better still, maybe she will acquire her own saris and kalidar angarkhas painstakingly created by 'the Boys'. Imagine that! Three generations draped by Abu Sandeep. Perhaps that really says it all.

SHOBHAA DE

about the photographer

Ram Shergill studied Visual Communications at Wolverhampton University. While working on a photographic project with Philip Treacy during his studies, he met Isabella Blow, and the meeting propelled him into the world of fashion. He became one of the key imagists of the avant-garde 'Cool Britannia' fashion scene and one of Britain's leading fashion photographers, working on editorial and advertising commissions for *Vogue*, *Harper's Bazaar*, *Tatler*, *i-D*, *POP*, *Dazed & Confused* and *W* magazine, among others. His many illustrious subjects have included Amy Winehouse, Naomi Campbell and the Scissor Sisters. He has also worked extensively with fashion designers, including Alexander McQueen.

His photographs are influenced by memories of his early childhood. Poor sight meant that he fantasized a rose-tinted perfect world in which everything was beautiful; once his vision had been corrected, his surroundings were no longer a blur but rather a visual treat. During his college years he became transfixed by photography books, in which he would lose himself and imagine that he was part of the images he was studying. He also began to visit art galleries and discovered the work of Cecil Beaton, Horst P. Horst, Richard Avedon and Irving Penn, whose elegant aesthetic inspired him.

His own photographs have been exhibited at the Whitechapel Art Gallery and the Victoria and Albert Museum, both in London. He works internationally, particularly in Europe and India. He is also the founder and publisher of *Drama Magazine*, based around fashion and performance.

about the writer

Gayatri Sinha is an art critic and curator based in New Delhi. Her primary areas of enquiry are around the structures of gender and iconography, media, economics and social history. As a curator, her work has cited the domains of photography and lens-based work from archival and contemporary sources. She has edited *Voices of Change: 20 Indian Artists* (Marg Publications, 2010), *Art and Visual Culture in India: 1857–2007* (Marg Publications, 2009), *Indian Art: An Overview* (Rupa Books, 2003), *Woman/Goddess* (Multiple Action Research Group, 1998) and *Expressions and Evocations: Contemporary Indian Women Artists of India* (Marg Publications, 1996).

She has curated extensively in India and abroad, including at the India Art Summit and the Korean International Art Fair (2009), Newark Museum and the Minneapolis Institute of Art (2008–9), Fotografie Forum Frankfurt (2006), National Museum, New Delhi (2004), Festival of India in Bangladesh (1997) and the National Gallery of Modern Art (1996). As an art critic, she wrote a column for the *Indian Express* and *The Hindu*, and has written monographs on the artists Krishen Khanna and Himmat Shah.

She has also lectured widely on Indian art, including at the Centre Pompidou, Paris; TrAIN/University of the Arts, London; Tate Modern and Tate Britain, London; National Museum of India, New Delhi; Japan Foundation, Tokyo; and the Asian Art Museum, Singapore.

glossary

AARI *Straight running stitch, made with a hook-shaped needle.*

ANGARKHA *Long-sleeved, full-skirted tunic for men, generally open at the chest and tied in front with an inner flap (purdah) covering the chest; from the Sanskrit word 'angarakshak', meaning 'that which protects the limbs'.*

BADLA *Flattened gold or silver wirework.*

BANDHGALA *Regular-length jacket with front-button closing and high collar.*

BANDHINI *Tie-dyed fabric.*

BOOTI *Independent single flower motif.*

BOSKI *Variety of silk, relatively heavy in weight.*

CHADDAR *Piece of cloth, sheet or blanket; unstitched garment used to drape the upper body, also used as a dupatta (q.v.).*

CHIKAN *White embroidery, predominantly of floral patterns, traditionally executed on fine white cotton with untwisted threads of white cotton or silk.*

CHURI *Sleeve or trouser that is stitched overlong so that the excess length falls into folds and appears like a set of bangles (churis).*

CHURIDAR DOGRI *Style of tight-fitting pyjama ruched from knee to ankle; a cross between the sidha and the churidar pyjama favoured by the Dogras, erstwhile rulers of Kashmir.*

DHOTI *Cloth worn around the waist, passed between the legs and tucked in at the back.*

DUPATTA *Unstitched length of material for the upper body, traditionally worn by both sexes but now mainly worn by women as part of a shalwar kameez (pyjama and tunic) ensemble.*

GHAGRA *Gathered skirt, usually very flared.*

GOTA *Metallic ribbon in which badla (q.v.) forms the weft and silk or cotton the warp.*

JAAL *Floral trellis.*

JAALI *Intricate all-over-embroidered trellis.*

JAMDANI *Weaving technique traditional to the towns of Tanda, Jais and Dacca, used to produce figured muslins and organzas.*

JAMEVAR *Trade name for woven or embroidered Kashmir shawls.*

KAIRI *Mango-shaped motif.*

KALIDAR KURTA *Traditional panelled tunic with a placket, worn over churidar or pants.*

KANJEEVARAM SARI *Handwoven silk sari from the Kanchipuram district, Tamil Nadu.*

KASAB *Gold thread.*

KHADI *Indian hand-spun and hand-woven cloth.*

KHAKA *Artwork used for embroidery.*

KURTA CHURIDAR *Outfit consisting of a loose, stitched garment worn by men and women, most commonly described as a tunic (also known as a kameez), worn with a style of tight-fitting pyjama ruched from knee to ankle.*

KURTI *Shorter version of the kurta (q.v.), worn by women.*

LEHENGA *Skirt, particularly associated with weddings.*

LEHERIYA *Traditional Rajasthani dyed pattern, resembling a wave, which goes diagonally across the cloth.*

MARODI *Hand-embroidery zardozi stitch with twisted threads.*

PAAN *Leaf-shaped motif.*

PALLOO *Decorative border at one or both ends of a length of fabric, usually a sari, odhani (veil-cloth) or patka (girdle).*

PATTI *Leaf pattern.*

RESHAM *Silk thread.*

SARI *Strip of unstitched cloth worn by females draped over the body; the length of a traditional Indian sari is five and a half yards.*

SHERWANI *Formal knee-length coat fitted to the waist.*

TANCHOI *Figured silk with multiple supplementary weft threads that create a heavy, densely patterned fabric.*

ZARDOZI *Gold thread embroidery, sometimes using mirrors and precious or semi-precious stones.*

acknowledgments

Thank you Amitabh Bachchan for your unflinching belief in us.

This book would not have been possible without the help, trust and support of Nita Ambani and Usha Mittal.

Thank you Jaya, Dimple and Amrita for always being a part of our lives. And thank you to Shweta and Rinke for being our very own Drama Queens.

Karan Johar, you're a star.

A very special thank you to Dame Judi Dench, Tabu, Twinkle Khanna and Sonali Bendre for being a part of our book. Salman Khan, Sussanne and Hrithik, Gauri and Shah Rukh, this book would have been incomplete without you.

We are blessed to have the love and support of Urmila Sondhi, Benu Kumar, Sabrina Jani, Lubna Khan, Mejoo Khan, Saudamini Mattu, Surya Mattu, Kichu Dandiya, Insiya and Brian Dhatt, Dr Rekha and Dr Ashit Sheth, and Dr Ramesh Aggarwal.

Thank you Abhishek and Aishwariya Bachchan, Nikhil Nanda, Pinky and Sanjay Reddy, Sameer Saran, Kaajal Anand, Alvira Agnihotri, Superna and Gaurav Motwane, Chandra Dalamal, Rekha and Vaneesha Mahtani, Harsha and Mehernosh Heeramaneck, Bina Kilachand, Hari and Mark, Lindy Hemming, Bob Starrett, Niharika and Ayub Khan, Salpi and Vishal Gandhi, and Pratima and Gaurav Bhatia for your help and support.

Shobhaa De, Vrinda Gopinath, Sharada Dwivedi, Aashish Hiramanek, Arjun Sawhney, Rukminee Guha Thakurta and Rohini Killough, your thoughts are special.

Thank you Ashok Salian for the photographs from our earlier shoots, and Dhun, and Suresh Cordo for the wonderful photographs. Thank you Sahil Mallik, Natasha Chib, Shreya Anand, Anurag Vora and Saikat Paul for making the shoots go smoothly.

Thanks to Craig Marsden, Clarabelle Saldana, Daniel Bauer, Kanta Motwani and her team from Kromakay Salons, Megumi Matsuno, Mehera Kohla, Mickey Contractor, Ojas Rajani and Subhash Vagal for making everyone look stunning, and to Tandy Anderson at Select and Versae Vanni at Next Paris. Thanks, too, to Andrew Hiles, Joshua Tucker, Philip Scott and Thomas Lakeman for all your help in the production of this book.

We also wish to thank Anupam Poddar, Devi Ratn – Jaipur, Devi Garh – Udaipur and Brighton Pavilion for letting us use your properties extensively during our fashion shoots. Thank you T. T. Barodawalla for the use of Tara Barodawalla's photograph. Thank you Tarang Arora of Amrapali and Rajiv Rawat and Mangalam Arts Jaipur for all your help.

We would like to give a big thank you to our team at AJSK. You have all been a part of our hard work and success. Especially many thanks to Afshan Mukherjee, Juhi Rais, Sanjay Mhatre, Umesh Mudaliar, Praveena Rai, Minna Singh and all our embroiderers and tailors who make our impossible possible. Thanks to Shehnaz Kidwai, Sita Sondhi and Parveen Abbasi for continuing the legacy of chikan for us, and to Flecka Pathwardhan, Triveni Dawar and Ruth Regan for rocking the sales.

The production of this book would have been impossible without the help of the team at Thames & Hudson. Thank you Gayatri Sinha for the wonderful text. A very big thank you to Graham Rounthwaite for the wonderful book design and all your help and time. 'Major! Drama! Book it! Cover! Fungru!' Ram Shergill, thank you!

Finally, we would like to thank all the people who wear our clothes and believe in our work. They have all contributed to making us who we are today.